Debating Special Education

Debating Special Education is a provocative yet timely book examining a range of criticisms made of special education in recent years. Michael Farrell analyses several key debates in special education giving balanced critical responses to inform policy and practice for the future of special education.

The book identifies possible limitations to the current special education knowledge base and provision. Farrell examines the value of labelling and classification, asks if intelligence testing may have detrimental effects and addresses a number of complex issues such as:

- how practitioners work within special education and if, sometimes, professionals may be self-serving;
- whether there is distinctive provision for different types of disabilities and disorders;
- inclusion as mainstreaming offered as an alternative to special education, and the challenges this presents.

The author's conclusion is that, in responding to these challenges, special education demonstrates its continuing relevance and strength. Presenting a range of international, cross-disciplinary perspectives and debates – which are vital to an understanding of special education today – and written in Farrell's typically accessible style, this book will be relevant for teachers of special children in ordinary and special schools, those on teacher training courses and anyone whose work relates to special education.

Michael Farrell is an independent consultant in special education. He has published extensively in the field; his books include *The Special Education Handbook*, *Celebrating the Special School*, *Key Issues in Special Education* and *Educating Special Children* along with a number of *The Effective Teacher's Guides* (all published by Routledge).

Debating Special Education

Michael Farrell

Routledge
Taylor & Francis Group

LONDON AND NEW YORK

First published 2010
by Routledge
2 Park Square, Milton Park, Abingdon, Oxon, OX14 4RN

Simultaneously published in the USA and Canada
by Routledge
270 Madison Avenue, New York, NY 10016

Routledge is an imprint of the Taylor & Francis Group, an informa business

© 2010 Michael Farrell

Typeset in Garamond and Gill Sans
by Swales & Willis Ltd, Exeter, Devon
Printed and bound in Great Britain by CPI Antony Rowe,
Chippenham, Wiltshire

British Library Cataloguing in Publication Data
A catalogue record for this book is available from the British Library

Library of Congress Cataloging-in-Publication Data
Farrell, Michael, 1948–
Debating special education / Michael Farrell.
p. cm.
Includes bibliographical references and index.
1. Special education. 2. Inclusive education. 3. Effective teaching.
4. Educational psychology. I. Title.
LC3950.F37 2010
371.9—dc22
2009044254

ISBN10: 0–415–56729–7 (hbk)
ISBN10: 0–415–56728–9 (pbk)
ISBN10: 0–203–85245–1 (ebk)

ISBN13: 978–0–415–56729–9 (hbk)
ISBN13: 978–0–415–56728–2 (pbk)
ISBN13: 978–0–203–85245–3 (ebk)

Contents

About the author

Michael Farrell was educated in the United Kingdom. After training as a teacher at Bishop Grosseteste College, Lincoln, and obtaining an honours degree from Nottingham University, he gained a Masters Degree in Education and Psychology from the Institute of Education, London University. Subsequently, he carried out research for a Master of Philosophy degree at the Institute of Psychiatry, Maudsley Hospital, London, and for a Doctor of Philosophy degree under the auspices of the Medical Research Council Cognitive Development Unit and London University.

Professionally, Michael Farrell worked as a head teacher, a lecturer at London University and as a local authority inspector. He managed a national psychometric project for City University, London and directed a national teacher education project for the United Kingdom Government Department of Education. His present role as a private special education consultant includes work with children and families, schools, local authorities, voluntary organizations, universities, and government departments in Britain and elsewhere.

His many books, translated into European and Asian languages, include:

- *Educating Special Children: An Introduction to Provision for Pupils with Disabilities and Disorders* (Routledge, 2008).
- *Foundations of Special Education: An Introduction* (Wiley, 2009).
- *The Special Education Handbook* (4th edition) (David Fulton, 2009).

Chapter 1

Introduction

Debating Special Education is intended for policy makers, academics, teachers doing higher level courses, professionals connected with special education, and local and government administrators. It should be relevant for many others who contribute to, and have, an interest in special education. Given the proposed wide range of readers of the book, and possible different understandings of special education, it is important to be clear what is meant by special education at the outset.

Consequently, this chapter begins with a very short definition of special education, then proceeds to elaborate its elements. To this end, the chapter defines general education. It then discusses the range of different types of disability and disorder such as 'mild cognitive impairment' and 'developmental coordination disorder'. The chapter proposes a broad definition of provision to include not only pedagogy, but also other aspects such as the curriculum and therapy. The aim of encouraging the academic progress and personal and social development of special children is explained. Finally, the content of subsequent chapters is outlined.

Special education: a short definition

As a starting point, the following brief definition of special education is proposed.

Special education concerns provision for pupils with disabilities and disorders comprising: curriculum and assessment, pedagogy, school and classroom organization, resources, and therapy. It aims to encourage the academic progress and personal and social development of special children.

The elements of this definition require elaboration in terms of general education, types of disability and disorder, provision for special children and academic progress and psychosocial development.

Education in general

To try to answer more fully the question, 'What is special education?' an obvious place to begin is by defining education more generally, then move to aspects, if there are any, which distinguish 'special' education.

Definitions of education tend to include reference to the content of what is taught and the way it is taught; the familiar distinction between content and method. A well-established definition along these lines is that of Peters (1966) who argues that education implies '. . . something worthwhile is being or has been intentionally transmitted in a morally acceptable manner'. Views of what constitutes worthwhile content may change over time and may vary in different cultures, but are likely to embrace skills, knowledge, attitudes and values (Farrell *et al.*, 1995, p. 70).

Methods of education are varied and extensive. Peters' (1966) definition emphasizes that the method used should be 'morally acceptable'. Those being educated should be able freely to examine differing views and information, and come to a reasoned conclusion. Where such features are lacking, it is more appropriate to speak of a recipient being indoctrinated, rather than educated. The 'intentional' aspect of Peters' definition distinguishes education from incidental learning. Education is likely to involve structured experiences that aid learning.

The method and content of education are evident in a definition provided by Soanes and Stevenson (2003). Content is implied by their claim that education involves, '. . . intellectual, moral and social instruction' (ibid.). In this conception, education concerns social and personal development as well as intellectual progress. Methodology is seen as, '. . . the process of giving or receiving systematic instruction' (ibid.). A wider notion of the methods of education has been suggested (Tharp, 1993, pp. 271–272), that includes modelling, questioning and task structuring.

In brief, education is considered to comprise an agreed content and acceptable methods and is distinguishable from indoctrination and incidental learning.

Types of disability and disorder

A further step in trying to define special education involves examining who is educated. Pupils participating in special education are identified as having different types of disabilities and disorders (Farrell, 2008b). These are considered in a later chapter on 'Classification'. Some disabilities and disorders imply comparisons with typical development and include cognitive impairment, communication disorders, reading disorder and developmental coordination disorder.

Others (for example, conduct disorder) have developmental implications and also suggest common agreements of expected behaviour. Traumatic brain injury is a category in the United States of America but not in the United Kingdom. It emerged because of concern that there should be particular recognition of the requirements of children after such injuries. More generally, different countries have slightly different ways of delineating disorders and disabilities, and may use different terminology, although there is considerable overlap.

Recognizing types of disabilities and disorders implies that the delineations can be justified. This is debated more with regard to some types (e.g. attention deficit hyper-activity disorder) than others (e.g. profound cognitive impairment) (Farrell, 2008b, chapter 1 and passim). Recognizing disabilities and disorders also implies ways of iden-tifying them. This may involve applying criteria relating to categorical classifications such as those in the *Diagnostic and Statistical Manual of Mental Disorders Fourth Edition Text Revision (DSM-IV-TR)* (American Psychiatric Association, 2000). It could include pae-diatric screening or reference to some agreed benchmark of typical development. Detailed assessment of the child, and of the impact of the disability or disorder, is expected to enable parents, teachers and others to consider possible implications for learning and development.

Provision for special children

By 'special children', is meant children with disabilities and disorders who are deemed to require special education. The United States Department of Education has defined special education as, 'specially designed instruction . . . to meet the unique needs of a child with a disability' (United States Department of Education, 1999, pp. 124–125). But if special education is envisaged as broader than instruction, the term 'provision' may be preferable. Provision promoting the learning and development of special chil-dren comprises:

- the curriculum and related assessment
- pedagogy
- school and classroom organization
- resources, and
- therapy.

(Farrell, 2008b)

The school curriculum is sometimes understood as combining both the content and process through which learners 'gain knowledge and understanding, develop skills, and alter attitudes, appreciations and values . . .' (Doll, 1996, p. 15). The present book focuses on the curriculum as the content of what is taught and learned. This includes the aims and objectives of teaching and learning, and the design and structure of what is taught in relation to areas of learning and related programmes. The curriculum may be organized by subjects such as science or history or by areas like communication or social education. Some elements such as literacy, numeracy, computer skills, and prob-lem solving skills permeate the whole curriculum. A special curriculum may differ from a regular curriculum with regard to: the balance of subjects and areas; and the bal-ance of components of subjects; and the content of certain areas of the curriculum. The attainment levels implicit in some or all subjects may be lower than age typical.

Assessment may involve small steps to indicate progress in areas of difficulty (Farrell, 2008b, chapter 1). Assessments may require particular skills of the teacher and others such as very close observation of fleeting responses. They may require close multi-professional working, as with particular types of 'dynamic assessment' (Farrell, 2006a, p. 103).

Pedagogy concerns how the teacher promotes and encourages pupils' learning. It may involve individualized learning, group work, discussion, audiovisual approaches, whole class teaching, and other methods (Farrell *et al.*, 1995, p. 4). For special children, the teacher may present information emphasizing certain sensory modalities or encourage the pupil to use particular senses. A child with hearing impairment may learn sign language using visual, spatial and motor skills and knowledge, rather than hearing.

Approaches may be distinctive to a particular disability or disorder such as 'Structured Teaching' (Schopler, 1997) for children with autism. Some pedagogy is less obviously special. For pupils with mild cognitive impairment, there may be an emphasis on concrete examples of concepts and their use in developing more formal thinking. This can be seen as merely a 'more intensive and explicit' example of approaches used with all children (Lewis and Norwich, 2005, pp. 5–6), even though such teaching could be 'inappropriate for average or high attaining pupils' (ibid. p. 6).

School organization may involve flexible lesson arrival and departure times for some pupils with orthopaedic impairments. Safety has particular implications for pupils with attention deficit hyperactivity disorder, whose levels concentration may be variable and whose behaviour unpredictable. This may require higher levels of supervision than that for other pupils, in lessons where machinery or hazardous substances are used. Some pupils frequently absent from school because of medical conditions may benefit from home tuition and e-mailed work supporting home study. Classroom organization for pupils with profound or severe cognitive impairment may be informed by 'room management' (Lacey, 1991), an approach seeking to carefully deploy small teams of adults to ensure children's maximum participation.

Resources refer not just to learning resources, but also to school building and classroom design, furniture, and aids to learning and communication. School building design can assist access for pupils with orthopaedic impairment. Classroom design involves awareness of space, lighting, acoustics, and potential distractions and aids to learning. Furniture might include adjustable tables and adapted seating. Computer technology can use attractive stimuli to help the child recognize that his actions, such as pressing a button, can influence the environment.

Among physical and sensory aids is adapted equipment such as alternative keyboards. Resources for augmentative communication involve ways to augment partially intelligible speech. Those for alternative communication other than speech or writing are used to widen the scope of communication (Bigg *et al.*, 1999, p. 130). Cognitive aids include computer software encouraging responses; symbols for communication; and computer programs breaking tasks into manageable steps.

Therapy and care are broadly educational in that they lead to changes in behaviour, attitudes and self-valuing. Therapy helps promote skills, abilities and well being. For special children, it may include elements that are predominantly: physical (aspects of occupational therapy and physiotherapy); psychological (psychotherapy); communicative (speech-language therapy), or medical (drugs).

Academic progress and personal and social development

Like education generally, special education implies that what is provided enhances learning and development. Academic progress includes progress in school subjects and areas of the curriculum. This might be determined by curriculum-based assessments, standardized tests or informed observation. Development includes personal and social skills, high self-esteem, and concern for others. This may be assessed through observation in different settings; discussions between parents, teachers and others; interaction with the pupil, and other means.

Where special education is effective, it encourages progress in both learning and in personal and social development. There may be occasions when pupils do not progress and develop, perhaps because of a debilitating illness. Here, the aspiration might be to maintain levels of current functioning or to slow the rate of deterioration. (Please also see Farrell, 2001b, 2005.)

Chapter outlines

There is much to celebrate in special education (e.g. Farrell, 2001b, 2003a, b, 2004a, b, 2006a, 2008b; Kauffman and Hallahan, 2005). However, a range of criticisms of special education has been made in the past decades. The present text considers the most important of these, issues arising from them, and possible responses. These challenges inform the various chapters of this book as follows.

Chapter 2: Sociological criticisms

This chapter looks at the view that special education focuses almost exclusively on a 'within child' individual perspective to inform understanding and practice. In elevating individual approaches, it is sometimes argued, social perspectives are ignored or marginalized. The chapter considers the privileged place of an individual perspective in special education and the possible contribution of social orientations.

Chapter 3: Rights-based criticisms and contested values

A negative view of special education is that it segregates and oppresses children, ignoring the views of parents, children, and others. It is seen from this standpoint as socially unjust and divisive of the community. This chapter considers this position and the related values of equality of opportunity and social justice. Responses to this view are discussed, particularly focusing on the role of special schools.

Chapter 4: Post-modern criticisms

This chapter concentrates on three aspects of post-modern criticism. The first aspect is a post-modern view of scientific knowledge developed by Lyotard, leading to a questioning of positivist views of special education. The second challenge emerges from Foucault's insights into knowledge and power, which have been used to examine aspects of special education. The third concern relates to Derrida's approach of deconstruction, which has promoted questioning the stability of the meaning of discourses associated with special education. The chapter considers such developments and possible responses.

Chapter 5: Limitations of the special education knowledge base

It has been claimed that the knowledge base of special education is limited to psychology, psychiatry, and medicine and that special education is over-influenced by pseudo-scientific pretensions. This chapter examines three broad criticisms. The first is the suggested false legitimacy of special educational knowledge and the need to trust common sense knowledge and basic humanity. The second is to do with the perceived inferiority of special education research and overrated methods of assessment and pedagogy. The third criticism relates to the supposed role of reductionist epistemology in the separation of children. The chapter then outlines possible responses to these criticisms.

Chapter 6: The unhelpfulness of classifications

It is sometimes said that categorical classifications such as 'autism' or 'profound cognitive impairment' are unhelpful. This chapter considers the criticism that categories used in referring to disabilities and disorders are inappropriate and limiting and the view that non-categorical or dimensional systems are preferable.

Chapter 7: Problems with assessment

Assessments are regarded by some critics as part of the apparatus of separating children with disabilities and disorders. It is sometimes claimed that assessments of intelligence overemphasize hereditary influences, and lower expectations of children. This chapter examines such criticism and offers possible responses.

Chapter 8: Negative effects of labelling

It is argued that special educators and special education label children, which has negative effects. This chapter looks at the criticism that negative labelling associated with special education damages children's self-esteem, and lowers the aspirations of teachers, parents and others. It outlines how such criticisms might be met.

Chapter 9: Professional limitations

It has been intimated that special education professionals are typified by professional self-interest and isolationism and are too ready to use medication for children. The chapter looks at the criticism that often-unrecognized forces, such as professional self-interest or isolationism, and commercial interests are at work that run counter to the well-being of special children. It then proposes possible responses.

Chapter 10: Lack of distinctive provision

Some commentators suggest that different types of disabilities and disorders are merely classifications of children with no educational or other relevance. They do not lead to distinctive provision. This chapter examines the question of whether there is a special curriculum and pedagogy for special children. It then widens the consideration of provision to examine whether there are distinctive aspects of school and classroom organization, resources, and therapy in special education.

Chapter 11: The alternative of inclusion as mainstreaming

Inclusion as a euphemism for mainstreaming is defined. Some criticisms of inclusion are examined: the difficulty of maintaining inclusion as a primary aim, the claim that inclusion constitutes a liberation from oppression, illusions of equal opportunity, the weakness of claims of inclusion as a right and inclusion as fairness, and the lack of empirical evidence to support inclusion. Policy indications of the declining influence of inclusion are identified.

Chapter 12: Conclusion

At the end of each chapter is a 'summary statement', proposing a description or definition of an aspect of special education emerging from the chapter. The brief conclusion chapter draws on these summary statements to provide a description of contemporary special education.

The book ends with a bibliography and a combined subject and author index.

Summary statement

Special education concerns provision, for pupils with disabilities and disorders, comprising: curriculum and assessment, pedagogy, school and classroom organization, resources, and therapy. It aims to encourage the academic progress and personal and social development of special children.

Thinking points

Readers may wish to consider:

- the extent to which the proposed definition of provision conveys what is essential about special education;
- whether the range of further issues that have been raised are the most important.

Key text

Kauffman, J. M. and Hallahan, D. P. (2005) *Special Education: What It Is and Why We Need It.*
Boston, MA, Pearson/Allyn and Bacon.
This introductory book, in a short space, presents a strong case for special education and
explains some of its main features.

Further reading

Farrell, M. (2005) *Key Issues in Special Education: Raising Pupils' Achievement and Attainment.* New
York and London, Routledge.
This book, in a United Kingdom context, explores how pupils' attainment and progress relate
to special education policy and provision. It takes a broad view of progress to include both
educational progress and personal and social development.

Farrell, M. (2009b) (4th edition) *The Special Education Handbook.* London and New York,
Routledge.
This A to Z guide concerns special education particularly in the context of the United States
of America and England. It includes entries on concepts and terms used in special education,
descriptions of the main types of disability and disorder and related provision, the foundational disciplines of special education, and other areas. A thematic index guides those wishing
to read more systematically.

Farrell, M., Kerry, T. and Kerry, C. (1995) *The Blackwell Handbook of Education.* Oxford,
Blackwell.
In A to Z format and with a thematic index to help more systematic reading, the book concerns the very broad area of general education including basic concepts. The thematic index
has similar headings to those used in *The Special Education Handbook* mentioned above.

Mitchell, D. (ed.) (2004a) *Special Educational Needs and Inclusive Education: Major Themes in Education
Volume 1 Systems and Contexts.* London and New York, Routledge Falmer.
A selection of previously published articles from various journals indicating a range of
themes. These as brought out in the editors' introduction are: perspectives on the identity of
students with special educational needs, normalization and social role valorization, the over-
representation of different groups in special education, financing of provisions, the impact of
educational reforms on provisions, and international and national perspectives.

Reynolds, C. R. and Fletcher-Janzen, E. (eds) (2004) (2nd edition) *Concise Encyclopaedia of Special
Education: A Reference for the Education of Handicapped and Other Exceptional Children and Adults.*
Hoboken, NY, John Wiley and Sons.
This reference work includes reviews of assessment instruments, biographies, teaching
approaches, and overviews of learning disabilities.

Chapter 2

Sociological criticisms

Sociological views of special education sometimes criticize the centrality of an individual standpoint at the expense of social views. This chapter suggests that, while an individual perspective is likely to remain important, social viewpoints can and do make a positive contribution to special education. I look at possible layers of analysis drawing on individual and social perspectives and at implications for assessment and provision.

An individual perspective

Definitions of disabilities and disorders

An individual perspective is the most durable and established standpoint informing special education as typified in definitions and descriptions of disabilities and disorders. Profound cognitive impairment is defined in an individualistic way in both the United States of America where it is called 'profound mental retardation' and in England where it is known as 'profound and multiple learning difficulties'.

In the United States of America, the *Diagnostic and Statistical Manual of Mental Disorders Fourth Edition Text Revision* (*DSM-IV-TR*) (American Psychiatric Association, 2000, p. 42) defines profound mental retardation according to limitations in both intellectual functioning and in adaptive behaviour. It is associated with an intelligence quotient (IQ) range of below 20 or 25. However, IQ levels are interpreted with care, as they are not the sole criterion. Most children with profound mental retardation have an, 'identified neurological condition' accounting for the condition (ibid. p. 44). Impairments of sensory neural function are apparent in early childhood.

'Profound and multiple learning difficulties' is defined in government guidance in England. This states: 'Pupils with profound and multiple learning difficulties have severe and complex learning needs. In addition, they have other significant difficulties, such as physical disabilities or sensory impairment. Pupils require a high level of support, both for their learning needs and for personal care. . . . Some pupils communicate by gesture, eye pointing or symbols, others by very simple language . . .' (Department for Education and Skills, 2005, p. 7).

Identification and assessment

As well as definitions of disabilities and disorders having an individual orientation, identification and assessment also has a person centred focus. The identification of reading disorder (dyslexia) is based on observations and assessments of individual difficulties with reading and related skills.

The child may, when reading: hesitate over words; confuse letters with similar shapes such as 'u' and 'n', visually similar words like 'was' and 'saw' and small words such as 'it' and 'is'. He may omit small words such as 'to' and 'in'. The learner may make errors with semantically related words (reading 'cat' for 'dog'), polysyllabic words like 'corridor' or 'family', or grammar.

Identification and assessment tends to involve making a profile of such errors as well as other information about the pupil's reading preferences. Commercial assessments of reading disorder often sample component skills or necessary skills for reading. These include phonemic segmentation, that is the ability to segment language into phonemes (the smallest phonetic unit in a given language that can convey a difference in meaning). For example, in the word 'cat' the learner would be able to recognize and separate out the sounds 'c' 'a' and 't'. Another component skill of reading that may be assessed by a test is verbal fluency. For a fuller description and information on related biological and psychological aspects of reading and reading disorder, please see Beaton (2004).

Causal factors

Causal factors of disabilities and disorders tend to be related to the individual rather than for example to social or environmental influences. Regarding attention deficit hyperactivity (ADHD) disorder, concomitants that have been suggested are:

- genetic
- physiological, and
- psychological.

Genetic theories draw on evidence that ADHD is more common in the biological relatives of children having ADHD than in the biological relatives of children who do not. Twin studies show a greater incidence of ADHD among identical twins than non-identical twins. Studies comparing the incidence of ADHD indicate a greater probability of it appearing in parents and children when they are biologically related than if the child was adopted (Tannock, 1998).

Regarding physiology, ADHD may be related to dysfunction in the brain's neuro-transmission system, responsible for making connections between different parts of the brain. Brain imaging research with individuals with ADHD indicates abnormalities in the frontal lobes where systems responsible for regulating attention are centred. Reviews of neuroimaging studies suggest the involvement of right frontal-striatal brain circuitry. The cerebellum (part of the brain concerned with maintaining body posture and balance and coordinating motor activity) exerts a 'modulating influence' (Giedd *et al.*, 2001, p. 44). In 20–30% of instances, particularly in severe ADHD, the physiological features are caused by brain disease, brain injury, or exposure to toxins such as alcohol or other drugs.

One psychological theory is that characteristics of individuals with ADHD lead to difficulties with executive functions. These involve an individual's mental filtering and checking processes that are used to make decisions about how to behave. Executive functions involve: using inner speech; taking one's emotional state into account; and recalling knowledge from situations similar to one's current circumstances (Barkley, 1997).

Prevalence

Notions of prevalence of a disability or disorder tend to be individualistic. The prevalence of epilepsy is estimated to be about 1 in every 200 children and occurs more frequently among those with cognitive impairment. In the United Kingdom, it is estimated epilepsy affects 0.7% to 0.8% of all school children aged 5 to 17 years (Appleton and Gibbs, 1998). However, about a third of all epilepsies beginning in childhood will apparently disappear by the start of adolescence (Johnson and Parkinson, 2002, p. 2).

The individual nature of foundational disciplines

A range of disciplines can be identified that contribute to understandings of special education (Farrell, 2009a). These include perspectives drawing on the discipline of medicine (ibid. chapter 5), neuropsychology (ibid. chapter 6), individual psychotherapies (ibid. chapter 7), behavioural psychology (ibid. chapter 8), child development (ibid. chapter 9), and psycholinguistics (ibid. chapter 10).

To take one example, neuropsychology 'the study of brain-behaviour relationships' (Dewey and Tupper, 2004, p. xi) involves an understanding of brain structure and functioning. It seeks to link observed behaviours to areas of the brain used in carrying them out (Lezak *et al.*, 2004). Neuropsychology relates to aspects of disciplines, including neurology, cognitive psychology, genetics and biology. School neuropsychology applies knowledge of brain-behaviour relationships to school aged children. An aim of neuropsychology in relation to special education is to construct a pedagogical theory linking neuropsychological assessment data to effective intervention (Bernstein, 2000).

A school neuropsychologist is concerned with brain–behaviour relationships and their application in 'real life settings', for typically developing children and for children with disabilities and disorders (Hale and Fiorello, 2004, p. 4). Special education focuses on aspects of school neuropsychology relevant to the education and development of special children. The school neuropsychologist works with other psychologists, medical doctors and clinic staff, speech and language pathologists and teachers (ibid. p. 2).

However, not all foundational disciplines are predominantly individual in their orientation. Some forms of psychotherapy include the child's family or other groups (Farrell, 2009a, chapter 7). Observational learning within social learning theory (Bandura, 1977, 1986) includes 'modelling', which involves the child identifying closely with another person and learning from the way that person responds to situations (Farrell, 2009a, chapter 8). Sociological underpinnings focus on group and social understandings of disability and disorder (ibid. chapter 4).

Aspects of an individual perspective

Clearly, an individual perspective is influential in understanding disabilities and disorders and special education generally. This perspective provides definitions of disabilities and disorders, offers estimates of their prevalence, seeks to identify and assess them, looks for causal factors, and draws on disciplines that have an individual orientation. Those arguing for a social view of disabilities and disorders have made criticisms of the perspective. It is to these criticisms that we now turn.

Sociological criticisms of an individual perspective

Sociological criticisms of an individual view of disability and disorder include two inter related threads. The first is the proposal of an alternative approach or social model. The second is direct criticisms of the perceived limitations of an individual perspective.

An alternative social perspective of disability

Many views come under the umbrella of social perspectives. For example, a social constructionist perspective regards the 'world' as socially constructed. Social categories and social knowledge are seen as being produced by the communications and interactions between people (Berger and Luckmann, 1971). Social views applied to special education tends to attribute disability and disorder to environmental factors including the negative attitudes of teachers and others and the use of inappropriate teaching methods.

'Disability' is regarded as a socially created or constructed phenomenon additional to a person's impairment (Shakespeare, 2006, pp. 12–13) and can be seen as an interaction between the impairment and social influences. A social model may emphasize the way society includes or excludes disabled people (Campbell and Oliver, 1996). Impairment may be viewed as a biological feature, while disability is seen as the social response of oppression and disempowerment. Also, the term 'disability' tends to be used to speak very broadly about all kinds of disabilities and disorders. Because disability is seen as a product of social arrangements, it is believed it could be reduced and even eliminated. Given the perception that society is responsible for creating disability, changing that society would be expected to reduce disability. Mention is often made of disabling 'barriers' that, if removed, would reduce disability.

Those who hold a strong social perspective of disability (e.g. Oliver, 1995) have questioned what they regard as an inordinate emphasis on individual explanations and responses. This is related to the perceived inappropriateness of separate education for special children. If disability is largely constructed by society, the removal of barriers, it is believed, would reduce the disability to such an extent that separate schooling would be unnecessary. In this way, a link is made between a social view of disability and 'inclusion' in the sense of mainstreaming. Consequently, the view that special schools should be phased out and the education of all children should take place in mainstream classes has been debated under the remit of 'inclusion' (e.g. Jupp, 1992).

Limitations of an individual perspective

As well as proposing a social view of disability and disorder, those who take a social view relatedly point to perceived weaknesses in the individual approach, describing it as a 'deficit model' or a 'medical model'.

In an individual, perspective, disorder and disability in general, and types of disability and disorder in particular tend to be seen as 'within' the individual. This is sometimes referred to as a 'deficit model' because it may over emphasize what an individual cannot do rather than what he can. Individuals tend to be regarded as disabled, 'as a result of their physiological or cognitive impairments' (Drake, 1996, p. 148).

The emphasis is said to be on deficits and personal and functional limitations that are seen as the responsibility of the person concerned. These functional limitations are taken to be the cause of any disadvantages the person experiences. They can be rectified only by treatment or cure, according to this view (Barnes and Mercer, 1996). For critics of an individual perspective, it links notions of personal loss and personal inability to the idea of dependence on society. Such a dependency view is considered to negatively influence the identity of many disabled people (Campbell and Oliver, 1996).

An individual perspective may be regarded as a 'medical model' because of the framework of medical perception and terminology sometimes used such as 'diagnosis', 'aetiology' and 'treatment'. The *International Classification of Functioning, Disability and Health* (World Health Organization, 2001, p. 20), pointed out perceived negative implications of a 'medical model'. It is presented as viewing disability, 'as a problem of the person, directly caused by disease, trauma or other health condition, which requires medical care provided in the form of individual treatment by professionals'.

In relation to some disabilities and disorders, individualistic and medically orientated terminology and perspectives, it is maintained, are insufficiently questioned. Such acceptance, it is suggested, can help legitimize the use of medication when this may not be the only intervention or even the best course to take. The varying rates of use of medication for ADHD in different countries are a source of debate. One interpretation is that, in some countries, drugs are being overused. It has been suggested that medication may be being used as, 'short-term school performance enhancers for children' and, if so, this should be subject to open discussion rather than being masked behind an 'ostensibly medical condition' (Cohen, 2006, p. 19).

Responses to criticisms of an individual perspective

Responses to sociological criticisms of individual perspectives take three forms. Firstly, responses may be made to arguments of an individual approach implicit in the representations of a 'medical model' and 'deficit model'. Secondly, strengths of an individual view may be pointed out. Thirdly, weaknesses of the alternative social model can be identified.

Responses to medical model concerns

An individual perspective is sometimes caricatured as a 'medical model of disability' (e.g. Hurst, 2000, p. 1083), which can be misleading as the perspective reaches wider than the discipline of medicine. As already indicated, special education is informed not only by other disciplines essentially taking an individual approach, but also by perspectives taking account of group, family and social influences. The term 'medical model' is misleading in another way, as medical sociology recognizes the social context of disabilities and disorders (Bury, 2000).

This does, however, raise the issue of the use of medical terminology. Such terminology is appropriate with regard to some disabilities and disorders. Health impairments such as asthma, congenital heart condition, cystic fibrosis, diabetes and haemophilia tend to have known physical causes and are associated with medical treatments including medication. Educational responses and overall provision will take into account medical information and advice (Farrell, 2008a, chapter 9, 'Health impairments').

But with regard to some disabilities and disorders, critics holding a social view correctly question the use of medical vocabulary. In reading disorder, the use of such terminology implies a medically derived condition for what is essentially a difficulty with reading. This is not to diminish the importance of helping an individual who cannot read very well. But it is intended to question medical terminology being uncritically applied to an educational difficulty.

The use of the Greek term 'dyslexia', reference to 'diagnosis' (identification and assessment), 'prevalence' (a type of frequency), 'symptoms' (indications), 'treatment' (provision) and attendance at 'clinics' (often meeting rooms) seem to some to assume an unjustifiable medical basis. Similarly, Greek terms with medical overtones are sometimes used for developmental coordination disorder (dyspraxia) and mathematics disorder (dyscalculia).

Also, there are legitimate concerns about a medical orientation where it might lead to the possible overuse of medication, for example, for ADHD. In the United States of America, around 90% of pupils with ADHD receive some form of medication (Greenhill, 1998). In the United Kingdom, about 10% of pupils with ADHD are estimated to receive drugs (Munden and Arcelus, 1999), with fewer than 6% being administered the psychostimulant methylphenidate (Ritalin) (National Institute of Clinical Excellence, 2000).

Whatever the degree of effectiveness of methylphenidate, it is difficult to reconcile such discrepancies. One interpretation is that there may be over-zealous use of medication (Lloyd *et al.*, 2006). Many would agree the need for caution to ensure that factors other than medical efficacy such as commercial interests are not malignly influencing the use of medication for children.

It can be argued that an individual approach need not be a deficit approach. To include recognition of a child's areas of difficulty in any assessments of his strengths and weaknesses is no more a deficit approach than it is a strengths approach. To try to diminish or ignore areas of difficulty for the child is unlikely to be helpful. However, concerns about possible deficit thinking may remind professionals and parents to be vigilant that they do not come to see the disability or disorder as defining the child. Assessment and provision is likely to be useful where it is more holistic, taking into account what a child can do as well as what he cannot. (See also Farrell, 2004a, pp. 67–77 and 2004b, pp. 19–20.)

Strengths of an individual perspective

Strengths of an individual approach are also apparent. An individual standpoint can be important where the material basis of a disability or disorder is fairly clear. Traumatic brain injury gives rise to neurological problems that can be related to damaged brain areas. These include post-concussion syndrome, seizures and motor impairments. Injury can affect attention and memory, the visual system, executive functions, communications and behaviour (for a summary, please see Farrell, 2008b, pp. 140–145). Working out the implications for education involves close work between team members that include medical and educational professionals.

The approach of 'causal modelling' is illuminating some of the links between biological, psychological and behavioural aspects of disorders such as reading disorder and autism (Morton, 2004). This is essentially a way of trying to link different levels of explanation to provide a coherent and testable account of certain disorders.

Also, the individual model continues to produce evidence-based research that relates to particular disabilities and disorders (Farrell, 2008b; Fonagy *et al.*, 2005). This can indicate interventions that work for certain disabilities and disorders such as the provision of speech-language therapy and the inclusion of phonological teaching in reading where a child has a reading disorder related to a possible phonological deficit.

Weaknesses in the social model

The social model has been criticized. It is suggested that what started as a useful insight into the role of social factors in the experiences of disabled people has become an 'ossified' and 'increasingly ideological' view (Shakespeare, 2006, p. 13). Some definitions of disability are 'incoherent', giving a circular definition of impairment. They offer a definition of disability that does not include impairment and that concerns exclusions owing to physical and social barriers that apply to many groups considered socially excluded (ibid. p. 14).

A social view can close the door on understanding of disabilities and disorders that are specific. If disability is a social phenomena, it does not make sense to focus on specific disorders and disabilities for example to find if different types of provision such as pedagogy, curriculum, or therapy leads to better educational progress and personal and social development. Barrier removal becomes the sole approach to improving the lives of special children. It becomes irrelevant to know about the number of children with specific disorder, for example ADHD. Therefore, any concern that might be voiced about the possible overuse of medication for particular groups such as children with ADHD would not come to light.

Also, the distinction between impairment and disability is difficult to sustain as Tremain (2002) has indicated. Post-modern views suggest impairment is not a biological given untouched by social context. Impairment is itself part of the social and cultural 'discourse' of disability and disorder.

It has been suggested that impairment and disability are so closely inter-related, it is not feasible to separate their influence. Shakespeare (2006, p. 36) argues that a person with an impairment may simultaneously experience, 'socially engendered psycho-emotional problems' as well as 'impairment engendered psycho-emotional problems'. Each could lead to mental distress, but it would be practically impossible to separate the two. In this sense it is difficult to ague that an impairment is solely a physical entity and that social barriers and attitudes create a layer of disability in addition.

At its most muddled, the social perspective does not just try to act as a corrective to overly individual views of disability. It presents disability as a social construction insufficiently recognizing the permeating effect of the physical reality of disability. Shakespeare (2006, p. 53) suggests that the social model has come to a dead end, commenting, '. . . it hardly matters whether the social model is a system, model, paradigm, idea, definition or even tool. What matters is that the social model is wrong' (ibid.).

Ways forward

Inter-relationships between individual and social perspectives

In writing of perceived injustices to disabled people and how they might be generated, it is maintained that several mechanisms can be identified (Danermark and Gellerstedt, 2004, p. 350). These are cultural, socio-economic and biological. But it is argued that these levels cannot, on their own, help in an analytical approach to disability. Each can be seen as reducing phenomena to oversimplified levels, sometimes known as 'reductionism'. It is maintained, '. . . injustices to disabled people can be understood neither as generated solely by cultural mechanisms (cultural reductionism) nor by socio-economic mechanisms (economic reductionism) nor by biological mechanisms (biological reductionism)'. All of these levels need to be taken into account (ibid.).

Shakespeare (2006, pp. 54–56) takes a 'critical realist' perspective. This proposes that the experiences of a disabled individual arise from an interaction between factors 'intrinsic to the individual' and 'extrinsic factors' arising from the wider context. Intrinsic factors include the nature and severity of the impairment, personal qualities and abilities, and personality. Contextual factors include 'the attitudes and reactions of others, the extent to which the environment is enabling or disabling, and wider cultural, social and economic issues relevant to disability in that society' (ibid. p. 56).

Social constructivist contributions

One way of relating individual and social/cultural standpoints is through an interpretation of an aspect of the work of the Byelorussian psychologist Lev Vygotsky (1896–1934). Vygotsky's work can inform debates on the relative roles of individual factors and social/cultural factors in conceptualising disability and disorder and special education (Wertsch, 1985). The aspect of Vygotsky's work most often mentioned to inform a social constructivist theory of learning is the zone of proximal development. This concerns a child learning through instruction that is mediated by language. It is the distance between two levels of development, one actual and one potential. The first is, 'the actual developmental level as determined by independent problem solving'. The second is 'the level of potential development as determined through problem solving under adult guidance or in collaboration with more capable peers' (Vygotsky, [various dates]/1978, p. 86).

But enthusiasts for Vygotsky's social constructionist views tend to overlook his equally relevant and extensive work on what he called, 'defectology'. This work recognized the importance of biological (or 'natural') development as well as historical–cultural influences. For Vygotsky, the historical–cultural strand is internalized through the use of psychological 'tools': concepts, signs and symbols and language. It is superimposed on natural behaviour, substantially transforming it so that natural behaviour is embedded in the structures of personality.

Where there is a failure of biological function, another line of development, helped by socio-cultural 'tools', can come into effect. This enables other biological functions to circumvent the weak point and form a psychological superstructure over it, so the disability does not dominate the whole personality (Knox and Stevens, 1993, pp. 12–13, translators introduction, paraphrased). Maintaining that a child with a disability has developed differently from peers, Vygotsky, ([1927]/1993, p. 30) proposes a compensatory and adaptive perspective.

In this perspective, the child's development represents a creative physical and psychological process. This involves the shaping of the child's personality through restructuring adaptive functions and forming new processes brought about by the disability. This creates new, roundabout paths for development (Vygotsky, [1927]/1993, p. 34, paraphrased). But, while typical development can be conditioned by culture spontaneously and directly, atypical development cannot (ibid. p. 42, paraphrased). Therefore, special pedagogy is necessary because cultural development in a special child involves a particular line of development, guided by distinctive l aws, and with specific difficulties and means of overcoming them (ibid. p. 43 paraphrased).

A consideration of aspects of Vygotsky's work informs special education by helping raise the importance of language and mediation in aiding learning, and indicating possible inter- relationships of biological and social-cultural factors.

Layers of analysis

An understanding of disabilities and disorders and of special education can be developed by regarding perspectives as inter related layers of analysis and by developing related approaches to assessment and practice. The approach maintains an individual view, but draws also on other perspectives.

Analysis of disability and disorder in the context of special education in a mainstream school might involve a review informed by a social perspective. This could examine the potential barriers to learning and development, such as participatory and attitudinal barriers. The review could include examining several features of the school and its procedures. Participation could be improved through computer technology. Any attitudes of parents and adults working in the school that might lead to low expectations limiting the progress and development of pupils could be challenged. All these developments and improvements could be characterized as removing 'barriers'.

Strictly speaking, a social constructionist perspective concentrates on social and attitudinal barriers. However, physical barriers could also be examined to the extent that they inhibit participation and social interaction. Physical access to areas of the school building could be reassessed and enhanced. For children with visual impairment, tactile maps and other aids to orientation in the school could be improved and extended.

Social constructivist perspectives can help draw attention to the mediating role of language in learning. Aspects of Vygotsky's work can indicate the possible interactions of biological and social/cultural factors. In the classroom, the idea of a zone of proximal development may inform teaching. Where a child does not have spoken language, but can communicate symbolically in other ways, for example, by sign language or symbols, a similar scaffolding principle might be used. (This is not made explicit in Vygotsky's work.)

All the layers considered so far recognize the material reality of disability and disorder. The concern often is that overemphasizing this material reality can be restrictive, as in an individual perspective. But such a perspective allows understandings and interventions to be developed that can encourage learning and development. The development of behavioural orientated approaches and visual cues for children with autism is an example.

Conclusion

Both individual and social perspectives contribute to understanding disability and disorder. They can also inform a systematic approach to assessment and provision in special education. An individual perspective underpins much of classification, identification, assessment and provision in special education. But this does not preclude insights from social views. Indeed special education is strengthened by this contribution.

Summary statement

Special education draws on individual and social perspectives to inform under-standing and practice.

Thinking points

Readers may wish to consider:

- the extent to which the individual and social perspectives represent the main approaches to disability and disorder;
- the degree to which individual and social perspectives might be theoretically exclusive or compatible;
- the practical implications for schools of drawing on both individual and social perspectives.

Key text

Shakespeare, T. (2006) *Disability Rights and Wrongs*. London and New York, Routledge.
   A well-argued and subtle analysis of issues in disability studies pointing up the weaknesses of the social model. It opens up a range of issues such as responses to charity that take on different complexions when the rigidity of the social model is discarded.

Further reading

Barton, L. (ed.) (2006) *Overcoming Disabling Barriers: 18 Years of Disability and Society*. New York/ London, Routledge.
   This comprises articles from the journal *Disability and Society*. The first section, on disability studies, includes articles on the social model of disability.
Karpov, Y. V. (2005) *The Neo-Vygotskian Approach to Child Development*. New York, Cambridge University Press.
   This book critically presents Neo-Vygotskian attempts to integrate child development (cognitive, motivational and social) with the role of children's activity as mediated by adults in development.
Thomas, C. (2007) *Sociologies of Disability and Illness: Contested Ideas in Disability Studies and Medical Sociology*. New York/ London, Palgrave Macmillan.
   The book sets out in historical context, some the areas of overlap and differences in medical sociology and disability studies.

Chapter 3

Rights-based criticisms and contested values

Could go further way round!

A criticism of special education, where it involves the separate education of children for example in special schools, is that it is denying a right to education in the mainstream.

The question of rights may be related to discussions about equality of opportunity and social justice. This chapter looks at rights, equality of opportunity, and social justice. It examines the view that special education generally and special schools in particular deny rights, run counter to equality of opportunity and are socially unjust. Possible responses to these perspectives are discussed.

Human rights

The inflation of rights

What is a 'right'? Briefly, a 'right' to do something (for example, to publicly state one's views) implies that what is proposed is not wrong and that others accept that it would be wrong to interfere. This has been described as conditions of 'permissibility' and of 'prohibition of interference' (Mautner, 2000, p. 487, definition 3). I have a right to free speech if it is not wrong to speak freely and if others agree they should not interfere. For every right, it can be argued, there is a commensurate responsibility placed on others not to prevent the exercise of that right. Any individual or group in isolation, therefore, cannot announce a right in the sense described. It has to be agreed and negotiated with others within the fabric of a society at a particular time.

Some years ago, on the international stage, in recognition of potential inflation of rights, attempts were made to ensure any new rights are fundamental. Alston (1984) suggested that new international 'human rights' be subject to a kind of quality control by the United Nations General Assembly. Adopted in 1986, a United Nations resolution set out compliance criteria for international human rights instruments. These included that they should, 'be of fundamental character and derive from the inherent dignity and worth of the human person'.

Inflated lists of supposed rights seem to perceive them as a quality that an individual somehow carries round as part of himself as a rights' bearer. Glendon (1991) raises the concern that the ever-expanding catalogue of rights may trivialize any core rights that may exist, while doing little to advance the numerous further causes that have been claimed to be rights.

Yet the language of human rights shows little sign of moderating or abating. (Please see further examples in Farrell, 2009a, chapter 3; and the sections on inclusion as a supposed right in chapter 11 'Inclusion as an alternative to special education' in the present volume.)

Rights and special education

In recent years, the notion of rights has become increasingly discussed and the language of rights has been used to argue for particular positions. It has been claimed that the moral basis for 'inclusion' in the sense of mainstreaming education is one of rights (Gallagher, 2001). When pupils are educated in special schools, it has been maintained, a basic human right to be educated with others is denied. Special schools are 'segregating' and as such are seen as inherently wrong. Thus a principled position based on apparent rights can be taken that special schools should be closed and that all education should take place in schools for all children.

Anyone disagreeing with comprehensive education may be mentioned in the same breath as the Nazis in Germany or the apartheid regime of South Africa. The word, 'segregating' is used rather than 'separate' schooling to underline the perceived moral indignity of special schooling. It is said, 'When we come to segregating those who have special needs, we should not flinch from asking ourselves who (sic) it is that we are attempting to protect' (Jupp, 1992). We are reminded, 'Adolf Hitler separated the Jews, those who had a disability and homosexuals from other Germans, in order to protect the master race from, 'impurities'. South Africa segregated its blacks in order to protect its whites' (ibid.).

It has been said, rights enable individuals to '. . . demand what is our due without having to grovel, plead or beg' (Bandman, 1973). More recently, it has been suggested that a 'moral commitment' is needed to include all children into a single education system. Furthermore, it is said, this should be translated into 'political *rights*' achieved by supporting the parents of children with special needs as they 'struggle to empower themselves' (Oliver, 1995, italics added).

It is claimed 'There is a growing consensus throughout the world that all children have the *right* to be educated together' (Wertheimer, 1997, italics added). There is 'struggle to abolish segregated education' which 'denies children with disabilities the *right* to be part of mainstream schooling . . .' (ibid. italics added). Furthermore, 'The *rights* enshrined in the United Nations Convention are applicable to all children without discrimination including the *right* to education on the basis of equal opportunity' (ibid. italics added). Terms such as 'struggle' are used to convey the effort needed to achieve liberation from perceived oppression. The word 'enshrined' suggests a sacred pedestal on which rights are placed so that anyone questioning them is immediately perceived as sacrilegious.

The *United Nations Convention on the Rights of the Child* (United Nations, 1989) states in article 1 paragraph 1, that, 'States shall respect and ensure the rights set forth in the present Convention to each child within their jurisdiction without discrimination of any kind, irrespective of the child's or his or her parent's or legal guardian's race, colour, sex, language, religion, political or other opinion, national, ethnic, or social origin, property, disability, birth, or other status.' Article 12 says, 'States Parties shall assure to the child who is capable of forming his or her own views the right to express those views freely in all matters affecting the child, the views of the child being given due weight in accordance with the age and maturity of the child.'

Such statements as article 1 and 12 quoted above may be quoted by those supporting mainstreaming as suggesting that separate education, for example in special schools, breaches human rights. However, it will be seen that these statements do not support such a view. Indeed, the articles are conversant with quite a different interpretation. In article 12 for example, the child who expresses a preference for separate schooling say in a special school, should have 'due weight' given to his views. Article 1 indicates that the child's rights should be respected and ensured 'without discrimination' irrespective of his disability. This includes the rights expressed in other articles including the right to express a preference such as a preference for a special school.

The United Nations Educational, Scientific and Cultural Organization's *The Salamanca Statement and Framework for Action on Special Needs Education* is sometimes presented as providing unequivocal support for inclusive (mainstream) education. Yet section 3, paragraph 2 is rarely quoted. This is because it qualifies the enrolment of children in regular schools by stating this is to be done only if there are no compelling reasons to act otherwise. The Salamanca Statement says: 'We call upon all governments and urge them to . . . adopt as a matter of law or policy the principle of inclusive education, enrolling all children in regular schools, unless there compelling reasons for doing otherwise'. Signatories to the statement are, of course, at perfect liberty to set out compelling reasons not to comply. These include practicability, cost and the incompatibility of inclusion with the educational needs of all children.

Supposed rights are becoming more insistent as fewer people agree with them. It is said that in the 'struggle' for disabled people for inclusion, 'special, segregated education has no role to play' (Oliver, 1995). In 'reconstructing' the responses of schools and teachers, it is stated, 'Reconstruction on the basis of rights to inclusion suggests that there *must* be changes in the ethos of the school which *must* mean the school becomes a welcoming environment for all children . . .' (ibid. italics added). It is affirmed that there are 'rights' such that no one else is allowed to question them. Reconstruction means that, '. . . there is no questioning of the rights of any to be there . . .' (ibid.).

Responses to increases in supposed rights

In this context there are two choices. One can ignore the avalanche of supposed rights as no more than people insisting that they want something and that others should concur. Alternatively, one can join the melee and create more rights. In the second context, the notion that there are 'rights' for children to be educated together can have no greater claim to adherence than a claim that children have the 'right' to educated separately.

The 'right' to be educated in an ordinary school, is claimed by those who regard inclusion as synonymous with mainstreaming. Within disability rights approaches some deaf adults argue that deaf children have a right to learn a sign language as their first language to be part of the deaf culture (Hornby *et al.*, 1997, p. 3). The 'right' for deaf children to be educated in a special school is claimed by those who believe that deaf people are a linguistic minority whose form of communication aught to be encouraged by their being educated together. More generally, numerous parents and pupils prefer to exercise their 'right' that their child be educated in a special school. Parents fight for the continuation of their local special schools for this reason (Farrell, 2006a).

A further problem is that, if all children have a 'right' to be educated together and that right aught to be respected, then schools that separate children under any category are seen as denying human rights. There would be no separate schools for girls and boys. There would be no private schools for families that had saved to ensure their child was educated in smaller class groups than in taxpayer funded schools. Separate schools for different religious groups would become schools for children of all religions and none, following the principle of the hapless diplomat who proposed, 'Jews and Arabs should get together and sort out their differences like good Christians'.

Equality of opportunity

Equality of opportunity as an egalitarian aspiration

Rawls' (1971) 'justice as fairness' theory supports an egalitarian society and equality of opportunity and argues against social inequality. Conversely, Nozick (1974) claims that 'justice as fairness' proposals violate property rights and compromise freedom. Whatever the views of a general position on equality of opportunity, its implications with regard to disabilities and disorders are widely endorsed. Those who through no fault of their own lack the ability to achieve as easily as others would be given support necessary to help them do better than they otherwise might. This would be funded by individuals more fortunate in the level of ability they possessed, that is, property would be redistributed to try to make opportunities in society more equal.

The use of the term, 'equality of opportunity' is associated with an egalitarian aspiration for society. It can helpfully point to possible unjustified discrimination, for example, against individuals with disabilities and disorders.

Equality of opportunity and more equal outcomes

Supporters of comprehensive education may use the term 'equal opportunities' to suggest that all aught to have a chance to be educated in a mainstream school. In this perspective, special schools deny equality of opportunity to be included in mainstream classrooms. This applies also to other forms of separate provision such as within school units and separate classes. More specifically, separate provision may be presented as denying an equal opportunity for special children to participate with peers who do not have a disability or disorder. This might therefore reduce opportunities to learn social and personal skills from others.

The notion of equality of opportunity has problematic practical implications. It is assumed that the opportunity to benefit from any form of provision ensures that a child can and does benefit. This is captured in debates about equality of outcome. It is not always clear what is meant. It might refer to opportunity for equal access for example to a particular curriculum. Or the aspiration might refer to equality of opportunity that would lead to equal outcomes or at least more similar outcomes for all (Roaf and Bines, 1989).

Where it is meaningful to speak of equality of opportunity, then the expectation is that outcomes are improved for the children offered that equal opportunity. Where outcomes are unaffected or negative, then providing an equal opportunity to supposedly benefit from provision is meaningless. A child with autism may be provided with a place in a mainstream school classroom so that it may be said he is given an equal opportunity to benefit from inclusion with other children who are not autistic. But if he does not participate, or finds the environment threatening and distressing, it is unclear what opportunities are being equally enjoyed. The imagined equality of opportunity may be leading to poorer outcomes than might be found in, for example, a special school.

This seems to be the situation that leads parents to comment favourably on the opportunities offered by a change from mainstream to special school. The parent of an autistic daughter says of her child attending a mainstream nursery for two sessions a week, 'I used to dread taking and picking her up as it highlighted the enormous gap between her and children of the same age and I did not want to hear the feedback from the staff. I was made to feel I had a child who was beyond help.' Things changed dramatically when the child began special school.

The mother recalls, 'I will never forget picking her up on the first day. I arrived a little early to find the whole school in assembly. As I watched tentatively, I heard H's name being called out to receive a certificate for being such a star on her first day at school. I felt such a sense of pride and things just got better from that moment on. I started to think more positively encouraged by the positive feedback from the staff. The great thing was that H. was nothing unusual to them and they knew exactly how to deal with her' (personal communication, see also Farrell, 2006a, pp. 27–28).

Another difficulty with the notion of equality of opportunity is that, in emphasizing equality, it seems to preclude possible positive discrimination, for example, the provision of compensatory provision for special children. Such provision may not be correctly regarded as providing an equal opportunity to others for a child but as providing a much better opportunity. This also relates to outcomes because providing what are perceived to be better opportunities, so long as these can be seized, should lead to better outcomes for the child. This may be in terms of academic progress or in personal and social development.

Similarly, Hornby and colleagues (1997, pp. 68–90) analyse theory, research and practice with regard to special pupils using the term special educational needs or

'SEN'. They conclude, 'policies of increasing levels of integration for all children with SEN and of eventually including them all in their local schools should be abandoned' (p. 84). The authors argue for a continuum of provision including special schools, mainstream school units, and mainstream classrooms. Then the focus for special educators can return to optimising education for special pupils, 'rather than considering methods of achieving greater inclusion' (ibid. p. 85).

Kauffman and Hallahan (1995), in *The Illusion of Full Inclusion: A Comprehensive Critique of a Current Special Education Bandwagon*, regard the aspiration to full inclusion as 'illusory rhetoric'.

Social justice

The notion of fairness

Another frequently cited notion is that of social justice. It of often related to arguments about equality of opportunity and rights in that, if a child enjoys equality of opportunity and has his rights respected, then it is said this leads to social justice. This chapter has already alluded to problems with the concepts of both equality of opportunity and rights. But social justice is sometimes associated with another concept, that of 'fairness'.

It may be argued that this or that position is fair or the only fair one out of several alternatives. In claims for inclusion, it may be stated that it is 'fair' to educate all children in mainstream classrooms, and unfair to educate them in any way separately. This claim may be preceded with an appeal to respecting children. Mainstreaming is presented as treating a child with respect and separate provision as not doing so, because it is claimed it can make the child feel different and marginalized. Treating a child fairly involves not treating him differently to others. It is considered to be morally wrong to treat a child differently to others without providing relevant reasons for doing so.

Difficulties applying the concept of fairness

There is a difficulty with presenting mainstreaming as treating a child with respect and separate provision as not doing so. Such a position fails to recognize that the differential treatment may be morally appropriate or morally inappropriate. Real difference, such as that in the learning of a child with profound cognitive impairment or that of the behaviour of a young person with severe conduct disorder, can be acknowledged. Nevertheless, it does not necessarily lead to the child or youth being disrespected. As Barrow (2001, pp. 239–240) points out, acknowledging difference is not the same as lack of respect.

Regarding fairness, it can be accepted to be morally wrong to treat a child differently to others without providing relevant reasons for doing so. But the issue is whether the reasons given are relevant. These depend on context and require being established by independent reasoning. Whether behaviour is fair is determined by other substantive moral values and the facts of a particular situation.

Within this understanding, inclusion as a principle of school practice can lead to unfairness. A class may be designated and designed for pupils who have specified prior knowledge, skills or understanding. These have effectively become the criteria for admission. To take into such a class pupils who do not meet these criteria is unfair. This is because pupils are being treated identically for no good reason, which is as unfair as treating pupils differently for no good reason.

In such situations, it is not fair to base the treatment of pupils on irrelevant criteria. It is unfair to refuse to recognize differences that may be relevant to the most suitable and effective way of educating a pupil. Consequently, it cannot be morally right to adopt a policy of inclusion because inclusion is itself an unfair policy in refusing to discriminate on seemingly relevant criteria (Barrow, 2001, pp. 239–240).

Of course, inclusion can be justified in certain circumstances. But these have to involve further reasons other than simply claiming without warrant that it is fair and therefore socially just. The question of inclusion has to be placed in a specific context. This is likely to relate to some assessment of the ability of typical teachers and the purposes of educating pupils. Indeed, mainstreaming may be more relevant for pupils with certain types of disability and disorder than others.

There appears to be no universal answer to the question of whether inclusion is worth pursuing. Consequently, a more considered approach would be to take each issue on its own and try to resolve it from an educational and psychosocial developmental standpoint. Such a standpoint is 'optimal education' in which careful consideration is given to the child's educational progress and development (Farrell, 2006a).

Values relating to special education

The notion that the pursuit of rights points inevitably to comprehensive education is untenable. The individual 'rights bearer' nature of the current plethora of human rights and their potential to be flatly contradictory leads either to their being ignored or to the cynical ploy of inventing opposing human right to the ones being claimed by others. But special education can put forward positive values relating to equality of outcomes, and social justice. It also responds to the 'voice' of pupils and parents and offers service to the community.

Greater equality of outcomes

Values associated with special education include aiming for greater equality of outcomes. This may not mean equal provision, for example, educating all pupils in the same classroom. It may translate into different provision in terms of curriculum, pedagogy, and classroom and school organization. It may imply separate provision for some or all of the child's schooling either in separate classrooms, units, or special schools either day or boarding.

Education is assumed to be a given good and children, it is maintained, are entitled to the best education available. The best education is education that leads to the best academic progress in the broadest sense and to the best psychosocial development.

Determining whether a child is making the best progress and is developing well is not straightforward (see Farrell, 2009b, the entry on 'progress'). Where special provision leads to such outcomes, in the judgement of parents, pupils, teachers and others, then special education may be seen as the best provision.

Social justice

A further value is a commitment to social justice. This does not take quite the same form as for those arguing for inclusion. In that case, proponents argue that social justice is achieved when all pupils are educated together. In special education, it is maintained that social justice is best served where children are helped if they have difficulties. This may involve different elements of provision. Special education values children's education and development and nurtures it.

Respecting pupil and parent 'voice'

Another value associated with special education is that of respecting the positive views of pupils, parents, teachers and others connected with special educational provision. This applies to benefiting from special educational provision in a mainstream school or in a special school.

If the views of some who oppose the continuation of special schools are listened to, the views of those who take a diametrically opposite view need to be listened to also.

These include countless parents who value special education and who value special schools. They include numerous pupils who enjoy and benefit from special education in mainstream and special school. They encompass ex pupils who as adults look back with affection and gratitude on their experiences of special education. The views of professionals that devote themselves to special education might also be taken into account, if one can put aside for a moment the suspicion that they are all self-serving. (Please see Chapter 9, 'Professional limitations' in the present volume.)

Providing funds and service

Another value is that of service. It is sometimes suggested that any help is necessary for individuals with disabilities or disorders should come in some neutral way through government funds. This would distance the provider from the receiver so that those individuals who receive such support are not beholden to those individuals who have provided it. Such funding of course does not come from government but from the taxes of those who contribute to what the government chooses to spend. The government also has to have a mandate from electors to spend their money to support others who may need such support.

So there is a link between the giver and the receiver however uncomfortable that might be for those who present funding as yet another 'basic human right'. It has already been suggested that rights are not plucked from nowhere, but that they depend on others agreeing to a duty that supports the requested right. Of course, most people are happy to pay taxes to support those who require help. Special education is an instance where children may require extra money to be spent over and above what is normally provided for the education of a typical pupil. Given this funding and willingness of others to provide it, special educators aim to give service to their community. This involves supporting children who find it harder to learn than others, and helping their parents as necessary.

Conclusion

The intentions of those proposing equality of opportunity appears to be to encourage greater equality of outcomes such as better education and development. However, these gains are not always apparent. Human rights claims do provide a justification either for mainstreaming or for separate schooling. Social justice as fairness depends on justifying criteria for treating children either the same or differently and there is no moral superiority for treating children the same when there appear to be grounds for not doing so.

Summary statement: values

Special education strives for greater equality of outcomes for pupils, respects the voice of parents, children and others connected with special education, and is committed to social justice and service to the community.

Thinking points

Readers may wish to consider:

- the claims and counter claims regarding equality of opportunity and outcomes, rights, and social justice;
- what values might be justifiably associated with special education.

Key text

Cavanaugh, M. (2002) *Against Equality of Opportunity*. Oxford, Oxford University Press.
   A very closely argued reminder that even the shibboleth of equality of opportunity does not rest on a secure foundation. The suggestion of finding a 'good enough' position for anyone who is not equal however opens up further problems of definition.

Further reading

Armstrong, D. (2003) *Experiences of Special Education: Re-evaluating Policy and Practice Through Life Stories*. London, Routledge-Falmer.

Although this book does not provide up to date views of participants' experiences in special schools, it presents clearly arguments based on an oppression view of special education.

Farrell, M. (2006a) *Celebrating the Special School.* London, David Fulton.

This book includes chapters illustrating the views of parents and pupils who value special schools (chapter 3 and 4, respectively). Case studies are provided of successful and valued special schools, and supportive local authorities.

Hornby, G., Atkinson, M. and Howard, J. (1997) *Controversial Issues in Special Education.* London, David Fulton.

A forthright book looking at a range of issues. Chapter 5 examines policy, theory, research and practice with regard to inclusion.

Chapter 4

Post-modern criticisms

This chapter looks at aspects of the work of Jean-François Lyotard (1924–1998), Jacques Derrida (1930–2004) and Michel Foucault (1926–1984). It outlines Lyotard's conception of post-modern knowledge, Derrida's post-structuralist approach of deconstruction, and Foucault's notions of knowledge and power. The chapter examines criticisms of special education that have drawn on these elements, and suggests responses.

Lyotard's conception of post-modern scientific knowledge

Lyotard and post-modern scientific knowledge

French philosopher Jean-François Lyotard ([1979]/1984), reviewing the state of knowledge in highly developed societies, maintained the influence of post-structuralism had changed the nature of knowledge, requiring it to adapt. Scientific knowledge appears initially to have supplanted all other forms of knowledge ('narrative knowledge'), because scientific knowledge embraced a 'metanarrative' reflecting the values of humanism, which legitimized modern society. These perceived humanist truths include the view of history as progress, universal reason and the universality of the capacity for free individual action. However, in Lyotard's view, the spread of secularism and the diminution of political authority, are challenging the dominance of scientific knowledge and fostering suspicion of grand narratives.

Using the notion of 'language games' (Wittgenstein ([1945]/2001, e.g. pp. 7–8), Lyotard suggests how coherent narratives break up into many incompatible meanings; elevate the importance of particulars through diminishing the dominance of generalization and unification; and detach philosophy from the influence of scientific method. He also argues that clandestine power relationships shape modern thought. This points to a distrust of grand narratives as ideological constraints on individual thought and conduct. Scientific knowledge, he believed, gains its unjustified prestige and seeks its legitimacy from philosophical narratives (coming from German idealism typified by Kant) and political narratives (emerging from the French Enlightenment).

Yet for Lyotard, contradictorily, scientific knowledge depends for its legitimacy on philosophical and political narratives, which in science's view do not constitute knowledge at all. He argues this contradiction demonstrates science is inter-related to other discourses over which it has no privileged status. Furthermore, the waning credibility of German idealism and French Enlightenment thinking and the dependence of scientific knowledge on these for legitimacy weaken the legitimacy principle of knowledge. This blurs the dividing lines between different areas of science.

Post-modern science concerns 'undecidables' and paradoxes and evolve in a discontinuous way. Its 'model of legitimation' (Lyotard, [1979]/1984, p. 60) is based on reasoning that contradicts logical rules and is counter to usual and established ways of reasoning.

Post-modern views of science as 'intellectual posturing' were suggested when Alan Sokal, a Professor of Physics, submitted a spoof article to the cultural studies journal *Social Text* (Sokal and Bricmont, 1998). The spoof, 'Transgressing the Boundaries: Towards a Transformative Hermeneutics of Quantum Gravity', replete with false arguments and absurdities, asserting physical reality was a social construct, was accepted by the editors and published in 1996. (See also, Sokal and Bricmont, [1997]/1999.) More generally, Habermas (1980, 1985) criticises post-modernism for deserting the aspirations of modernity and adopting an eclectic irrationalism.

Criticisms of special education relating to views of post-modern scientific knowledge

Approaches in special education are often informed by positivist philosophy. This rejects pre-scientific thought including religion, metaphysics and superstition and takes the general view that science makes continuing progress. Knowledge is seen as based on sense experience and enquiry in the hard sciences. In the social sciences, a positivist approach concerns describing and explaining empirical facts.

A post-modern view of knowledge, as indicated, eschews a positivist view. Post-modern special education, it has been suggested (Gerber, 1994), is typified by a recognition, '. . . that social and historical forces contingently yet indeterminately impinge upon and shape the enterprise of special education, which itself is not the simple sum of children who have disabilities or their instructional experiences in classrooms' (ibid. p. 371).

Heshusius (1991), in criticizing curriculum-based assessment and direct instruction, in special education, suggests their underlying assumptions are parallel to the 'mechanistic, Newtonian paradigm'. This construction of reality, she argues, '. . . has been challenged by Einstein, and has been further shown to be fundamentally incorrect by Bohr, Heisenberg, Bohm, and other contemporary scientists and philosophers of science' (ibid. p. 317). More recently, Heshusius (2004, p. 205) has stated that the procedures of science were not 'divine intervention'. They were not constructed during the scientific revolution 'by indigenous peoples, by persons with disability, by slaves, by females, by children, or by poor and uneducated men and women . . .'

(ibid. p. 205). Science then is seen as 'a historically and socially embedded construction' (p. 206).

Such arguments focus on the contested nature of science and, from this position, maintain that special education, to the extent it depends on or draws on science, is failing to recognize the limitations of positivism. There are, of course, further arguments (some expressed by the authors mentioned in this section) that the complexity of human beings precludes the application of scientific procedures to them. However, these are not the focus of the present discussion. (But please see Chapter 5, 'Limitations of the special education knowledge base' in the present volume.)

Responses to criticisms of a post-modern view of knowledge in special education

Tolson (1998, p. 12) asserts '. . . without a common understanding, a common knowledge, prospects for coexistence among the world's many contending truths grows precariously faint'. In a similar vein, Gross (1998, p. 48) argues, that where in the past science may have offered 'false universals', these have been overthrown only by better science.

In this context, commentators such as Heshusius (1991) seem insufficiently to acknowledge that Newtonian physics and quantum physics continue to explain phenomena in their respective domains. No one has proved Newtonian physics 'wrong', but the limitations of the theory in specific circumstances have been identified and work is taking place on theories that address this. Also, Gerber (1994) suggests, Heisenberg's theories about the subatomic world '. . . are often misused metaphorically to argue the fundamental unsoundness of empirical methods of studying learning, individual differences, or education and schooling' (ibid. p. 376).

Kauffman (1999, p. 248) maintains post-modernism and deconstructivism present 'singularly egocentric' world views because one's own experience is the only one that is knowable. He argues the view that disability is a 'social construction' that one could 'eliminate (deconstruct, subvert, redefine . . .)' is 'seriously at odds with the science of exceptionality' (ibid.). That post-modernism is at odds with another perspective, does not, of course, of itself discredit post-modernism. Nevertheless, Kauffman's argument is also that the consequences of the views of some proponents of post-modernism could have unfortunate practical consequences for special children.

Post-modern perspectives would tend to miss opportunities afforded by evidence-based practice such as the use of behavioural approaches for conduct disorder, because they are founded on observation, explanation and rational assessment of their effects. Of course, attempts to undermine positivist aspects of special education do not have to claim that the foundations of the physical sciences are illusory. It can, instead, be argued that approaches suitable for the physical sciences cannot always be assumed to transfer to social sciences. One stumbling block for attempting a scientific approach to human beings could be the complexity of human conduct. Another difficulty might be the contradiction of being unavoidably within the human world and at the same time trying to assume a neutral perspective towards others.

Derrida's conception of deconstruction

Derrida and deconstruction

Algerian-French philosopher Jacques Derrida is commonly associated with 'deconstruction' involving a close analytic reading of a text to show it is not a coherent entity. Often, Derrida uses deconstruction to examine internal contradictions of philosophical discourse. It is difficult to specify approaches to deconstruction, because it involves an encounter with particular texts and modifies itself accordingly. Several of Derrida's early books demonstrate the process (Derrida, [1967]/1973; [various dates and 1967]/1978). But perhaps the best starting point is *Of Grammatology* (Derrida, [1967]/1977). Writing is regarded as 'all that gives rise to an inscription in general' and may include pictorial, musical and sculptural 'writing' (ibid.).

Derrida criticizes the way, in Western thought, meaning is structured as binary opposites such as presence/absence, being/nothingness, mind/body and speech/writing. The first paired term takes priority, for example, speech is privileged over writing. Speech (logos) is taken as expressing pre-existing ideas and as having, 'a relationship of essential and immediate proximity to the mind' (ibid. p. 11). As the speaker says the words, he and the listener simultaneously hear them. Derrida calls this belief in the self-presentation of meaning 'phonocentrism', a form of 'logocentrism' (ibid. p. 3). Writing, considered secondary to speech, lacks immediacy, and is at a distance from the speaker.

However, Derrida argues that such a binary opposition as speech and writing is illusory. Speech is itself structured by distance and difference just like writing. A word is characterized by distance in being separated into a signifier (phonic sounds) and a signified (a mental concept). Also, Derrida regards language as a system of differences where meaning is conveyed not by some quality of a single word, but by its difference from other words. Derrida calls this quality of speech to be characterized by distance and difference, *différence* which simultaneously indicates, 'the production of differing/deferring' (Derrida, [1967]/1977, p. 23).

Derrida's ([1967]/1977, pp. 141–164) reading of a particular text to destabilize binary meaning is illustrated by his chapter, 'That dangerous supplement', examining Rousseau's rhetoric on writing in relation to a desire for presence. Rousseau views writing as a less immediate therefore inferior representation of speech. Speech is a more direct expression of the self. But Rousseau finds it harder to express himself in speech because of intense shyness and finds his presence more faithfully represented in writing. His physical absence enables the presentation of truth, but his presence confounds it. Through his assumption of the need for absence, Rousseau is able to reappropriate the lost presence. But the attempted reappropriation subverts itself, because its starting point is not presence but a lack of presence. One cannot desire presence if one is already present. The starting point is therefore a *différence*. Writing and speech can no longer just be opposed, but have not become identical either. In fact, their identities are put in question. The logic of the supplement (both 'an addition' and 'a substitute') disturbs the balance of metaphysical binary oppositions. Speech is not just opposed to writing. Writing is added to speech and, at the same time, replaces it.

Speech and writing are neither opposed nor equivalent. They are not even equivalent to themselves but are their own *différence* from themselves. The doubleness of the word 'supplement' takes the signifying possibilities of the text beyond what is assumed to be Rousseau's conscious intentions.

Derrida does not deny the existence of relatively determinate truths or meanings, but seeks to see such things as the effects of a deeper history of language and the unconscious. As a political practice, deconstruction could question the logic whereby particular systems of thought, and their expressions as political structures and social institutions keep their force (Eagleton, 1996, p. 128). However, Foucault in the 1972 edition of *History of Madness* argues that Derrida's criticisms tend to be based on very small fragments of text and that deconstruction is 'A pedagogy that inversely gives to the voice of the masters that unlimited sovereignty that allows it indefinitely to re-say the text'.

Criticisms of special education derived from deconstruction

Danforth and Rhodes (1997) adapt aspects of deconstruction to special education. They suggest the acceptance of concepts such as 'disabled' hinders moves towards more inclusive schooling. This is, in part, because the concept 'disability' already assumes the identification and separation of one group of children from another. The authors argue that, in failing to contest the 'disability construct', inclusionists are effectively supporting the 'devaluation and stigmatization' of these students (ibid. p. 357). By developing an approach that questions the term, 'disability', it becomes possible to better advocate inclusion.

The authors see deconstruction as a way of prizing open the binary logic supporting the separation of children into 'moral and political categories based on "ability" and "disability" '(ibid. p. 358). Danforth and Rhodes (1997) attempt to deconstruct the binary pair 'ability' and 'disability'. They see the term 'ability' as the preferred or dominant part of the binary opposites and 'disability' as the less valued part. If the terminology of 'mental retardation' were rejected, they maintain, the construction of 'retardation' would be challenged and would lead to greater respect for children previously so labelled.

Danforth and Rhodes (1997) link 'deconstruction' and the 'social construction' of disability in a way that they recognize Derrida might 'baulk at' (ibid. p. 353). If disability is socially constructed unjustly, they argue, it can be 'socially constructed in a more respectful and egalitarian way if enough people steer the momentum of socio-cultural activity in that new direction' (ibid. p. 359). They suggest that both social constructionism and deconstruction assume different forms of disability, 'are not physical absolutes but social designations that are made by people in interaction and relationships' (ibid. p. 359).

However, deconstruction offers, 'a strategic, political means to promote local change in daily professional work' (ibid. pp. 359–360). If society 'somehow' lost the vocabulary of mental retardation, 'the constructed reality of mental retardation would no longer continue in its present form' (ibid. p. 360). The new terms that emerged could be politically and morally advantageous, allowing people previously labelled to be treated in a more respectful way.

Responses to criticisms of special education derived from deconstruction

Danforth and Rhodes (1997) maintain that, if anything (or everything) is socially constructed and language reflects and shapes this, changing language might change perceived reality. However, more pertinent to Derrida's deconstruction, they question the ability–disability dichotomy. The border between ability and disability is where, '. . . the assumed differentiation of the human categories . . . collapses on itself, where the practical logic of sorting children into distinct and meaningful types breaks down' (ibid. p. 360).

They criticize a diagnostic practice in which a parent and a school appeared to define reading performance differently and therefore disagreed whether the child had a reading difficulty (ibid. pp. 361–362). One party took a fairly mechanical view of reading and the other a more contextual one. They see the 'deconstructionist purpose' of this as pointing out that the two opposing definitions of reading, 'throw a paradigmatic monkey wrench into the process of diagnosing a reading disorder' (ibid. pp. 361–362). Yet the authors proceed from pointing out difficulties in always agreeing on a definition of reading performance to dismantling the assessment process with insufficient justification. Certainly, if an assessment involves criteria on which parties do not agree, they are unlikely to be in harmony on the outcome of the assessment. But this might suggest developing wider criteria or agreeing on the same criteria. It does not inevitably demand getting rid of the criteria.

Danforth and Rhodes (1997) attempt to deconstruct ability/disability by opening up its 'binary logic'. But the conclusion that the terminology of 'mental retardation' might be rejected lies beyond the remit of deconstruction. Their case might be better substantiated (though still open to challenge) through reference to labelling theory. The authors intimate that dropping certain terminology could lead to greater respect. But, if there was no use of such terms, who would know whether greater respect was being demonstrated and to whom? It is one thing to point to possible problems of logic in extended discourses, but quite another to suggest abolishing terms that might help identify children who could benefit from special education.

More generally, deconstruction can suggest how meaning in special education might be open to challenge. However, it does not point to direct consequences for special education. To leap from questioning the stability of meaning to banning words is difficult to justify and does not bode well for debate.

Foucault's work on knowledge and power

Foucault's work relating to knowledge and power

French philosopher and historian Michel Foucault examines the conditions that opened up the possibility of ways of knowing and the historically contingent practices that shaped them. He is concerned with periodic changes in perception and knowledge and the relationships between knowledge and power. Foucault analysed the historical development of forms knowledge regarding sexuality (Foucault, [1976]/1998), punishment (Foucault, [1975]/1991), medicine (Foucault, [1963]/2003), the humanities (Foucault, [1966]/2002) and madness (Foucault, [1961]/2006).

Through these historically situated sets of presuppositions of thought (epistémès), he argues, in a given period and in a given society, rational order is recognized. While epistémès are necessary for reality to be interpreted and discussed, they remain obscured. Through 'archaeology', these presuppositions can be unearthed, allowing one to examine fundamental structures of thought.

In considering how madness is made an object of knowledge, Foucault ([1961]/2006) traces historical transformations in conceptions of madness. With the development of scientific reason in the seventeenth and eighteenth centuries, sanity and madness became increasingly polarized, as the mad were seen as beyond Reason. In the nineteenth and twentieth centuries, psychiatry shaped madness as an illness subject to cure and normalization.

Examining the origins of modern medicine from the late 1700s, Foucault ([1963]/ 2003) suggests there was a shift in the structure of knowledge. This was from a taxonomic period to an 'organic historical' period, allowing the possibilty of a discourse about disease. Anatomy appears, therefore, more a product of a new structuring of knowledge than an uncomplicated empirical science, gradually recognizing what was 'real'.

One of Foucault's themes is 'power-knowledge'. Seeing power as all pervading and resistance as part of a related fabric, he is concerned with power and its relationship with discursive formations that make knowledge possible. For him, power refers to that which controls individuals and their knowledge, which enters discourses and attitudes and everyday life (Foucault, [various dates]/1980, p. 30).

Foucault ([1975]/1991) examines changes in Western penal systems in modern times. Concentrating on issues of power and of the human body, he maintains that prison is a new form of technological power, that of discipline. This power is evident elsewhere, including hospitals and schools. Foucault suggests there has been a move from penology, where there were clear links between crime and punishment, to overall surveillance. Discipline creates conforming bodies for the new industrial age, which function in various settings. These disciplinary institutions have to constantly observe the bodies they seek to control and ensure discipline is internalized as the bodies are moulded through observation.

Foucault states, 'there is no power relation without the correlative constitution of a field of knowledge, nor any knowledge that does not presuppose and constitute at the same time power relations' (ibid. p. 27). He suggests, 'The subject who knows the objects to be known and the modalities of knowledge', must be regarded as effects of 'the fundamental implications of power-knowledge and their historical transformations' (ibid. pp. 27–28). The processes and struggles that traverse and constitute power-knowledge determine the 'forms and possible domains of knowledge' (ibid.).

Among criticisms of Foucault's notion of epistémès, is incredulity about their pervasiveness. Steiner (1971) suggests, 'the whole idea of a visible "consciousness" appearing on Monday mornings or at the start and end of centuries, is a fatal simplification'.

Criticisms of special education drawing on Foucault's conceptions of knowledge and power

Insights arising in Foucault's work have been used to question the view of impairment as a natural phenomenon. As Tremain (2002) indicates, for Foucault, the materiality of the body is associated with the 'historically contingent practices that bring it into being, that is, *objectivize* it' (ibid. p. 34). Impairment and its materiality are 'naturalized *effects* of disciplinary knowledge/power' (ibid. p. 34). 'Impairment' has circulated in discursive and concrete practices as 'non-historical (biological) matter of the body, which is moulded by time and class, is culturally shaped or *on which* culture is imprinted' (ibid. pp. 34–35). Consequently, impairment has remained a prediscursive, politically neutral given. In challenging this one can 'identify and resist the ones that have material-*ized* it' (ibid. p. 35, all italics in original).

Historically shaped modern perceptions of the body emerging in the eighteenth century led to the creation of the modern body as 'the effect and object of medical examination, which could be used, abused, transformed and subjugated' (Tremain, 2002, p. 35). The clinical examination procedure led to the passivity of this 'object', and the investigative gaze 'fixed and crystallized' the phenomena it perceived as 'the body' (ibid. p. 35). For Foucault ([1976]/1998), this objectification of the body contributed to the new regime of power (biopower), whereby recent forms of power/knowledge led to increasingly comprehensive mangement of life.

The objectivization of the body interacted with 'dividing practices' (Foucault, [1963]/2003) instituted in the compartmentalization of ninetenth-century clinics and categorizing, distributing and manipulating subjects. By a process of division within themselves or from others, subjects are 'objectivized' as disabled, sick or mad and, through objectifying, procedures become attached to personal and social identity.

From the eighteenth century, proceedures and operations or 'technologies' coalesced around the objectivization of the body. One of these, 'discipline', includes instruments, techniques and procedures of power to produce a body that can be used, transformed and improved. This exercise of power involves guiding the possibilties of conduct. However, it is self-concealing allowing, 'the naturalization and legitimation of the discursive formation in which they circulate' (Tremain, 2002, p. 36). Hegenomic power structures (structures maintaining power that are invisible to those held down because of their pervasiveness) are made possible through the production of apparent acts of choice by the subject. Normality and normalization are central to biopower, allowing the identification of subjects by others and themselves in ways that make them governable.

Allen (1996) also relates Foucault's ideas directly to special education. She contends that research into special children educated in mainstream schools tends to indicate little about their school experiences. Foucault's methodology of examining discourses and his analysis for example of medicine and madness are thought to provide alternatives. Allen maintains that Foucault can provide strategies for understanding how discourses on 'special needs' construct pupils' experiences in mainstream schools and constructs their identities as 'subjects and objects of knowledge' (ibid.).

Allen draws on Foucault's ([1975]/1991) notions of surveillance through hierarchical observation (ibid. pp. 170–177), normalizing judgement (pp. 177–184), and the examination (pp. 184–194). She suggests (Allen, 1996) that, in special education, hierarchical observation can be identified in the higher staffing ratios special children attract. Similarly, normalizing judgements are evident in the way special children are 'defined in relation to normality' (ibid. p. 223). The 'examination' is seen as relating to assessment, determining whether a child has a disability or disorder, leading to entitlement to special education. Allen suggests Foucault's view of power relationships provides the opportunity of looking for special pupils 'challenging the identities they are given or opting for alternative experiences' (ibid. p. 225).

Responses to criticisms of special education derived from Foucault's views of knowledge and power

Allen (1996) focuses on the power knowledge fabric of special education, arguing that individuals should show resistance to counter the possibility of assuming an identity shaped by others. There are, however, other power knowledge structures and fabrics around special children. There are forces with support from lobby groups, some researchers and academics, 'critical' psychiatrists and psychologists and others pressing for the mainstreaming of special children. Allen does not make it clear why the power pervading special education might be resisted rather than the power that pervades efforts to encourage 'integration'. In other words, it appears that a value judgement is embedded in her analysis, assuming that the power knowledge associated with special education should be resisted while power-knowledge structures supporting mainstreaming are accepted.

In her discussion of the 'examination', Allen (1996) claims that, when a formal assessment is made, there is usually little doubt about the 'special educational need' although 'the notion of difference is itself socially constructed' (ibid. p. 224). She states that the multi-disciplinary assessment gathering information about the child and his home background is 'primarily a political and social process' (ibid.). No justification is provided in the article for these statements. It could be argued that such processes and the provision of special education might be helpful and lead to the child experiencing better progress and development, rather than being simply 'marked out for perpetual surveillance' (ibid.).

Similar reservations can be held about other research and speculation, drawing on Foucault's conception of power-knowledge. If the matrix of power-knowledge pervades every aspect of social life, there needs to be some further justification of why one set of power-knowledge relationships might be challenged rather others. Also, if a set of power-knowledge relationships is considered malign, researchers and commentators might explain why, or produce evidence of ill effects. The belief that everything is 'socially constructed' does not, of itself, constitute a form of criticism.

Nevertheless, studies drawing on aspects of Foucault's views may point to a greater awareness of discourse and power-knowledge structures. Awareness of power/

knowledge relationships might encourage professionals increasingly to recognize the importance of pupils' views.

Conclusion

Perhaps the weakest criticisms of special education are those seeking to undermine its positivist foundations by attacking the tenets of the physical sciences. Special education draws on a positivist perspective to seek evidence-based provision. Deconstruction can suggest how the meaning of some terms in special education might be unstable, but perceived consequences for special education are unclear. The notion that certain labels should be no longer used does not emerge from deconstruction, and arguments relating to labelling theory might support the case better. Foucault's ideas suggest professionals become more aware of possible knowledge and power aspects of their roles.

Summary statement: post-modern criticisms

Special education draws on evidence-based approaches, professionals seek to be aware of the power and knowledge implications of their roles, and efforts are made to elicit and respond to pupil's views and feelings.

Thinking points

Readers may wish to consider:

- the extent to which the aspects of post-modern thought that have been selected for the chapter represent central themes;
- the degree to which these post-modern considerations form credible criticisms of special education;
- the convincingness of the responses to the post-modern criticisms of special education.

Key text

Corker, M. and Shakespeare, T. (eds) (2002) *Disability/Postmodernity: Embodying Disability Theory.* London, Continuum.
A stimulating book, mainly relating to notions of disability.

Further reading

Derrida, J. ([1967]/1976) *Of Grammatology.* Baltimore and London, The Johns Hopkins University Press (translated from the French by Gayatri Chakravorty Spivak).

Includes a critical examination of the prioritization of speech over writing.

Foucault, M. ([1969]/2002) *The Archaeology of Knowledge*. London, Routledge Classics (translated from the French by A. M. Sheridan-Smith).

A theoretical account of the processes of discovering historically underpinning modes of thought.

Foucault, M. ([1975]/1995) *Discipline and Punish: The Birth of the Prison*. New York, Vintage Books (translated from the French by Allan Sheridan).

Considers not only the development of punishment, but also of discipline in various settings including schools. The parts of the book concern: torture, punishment, discipline and prison.

Lyotard, F. ([1979]/1984) *The Postmodern Condition: A Report on Knowledge*. Manchester, Manchester University Press (translated from the French by G. Bennington and B. Massumi). This report commissioned by the Quebec government is probably Lyotard's most widely known work.

Chapter 5

Limitations of the special education knowledge base

The knowledge on which special education draws has been developed over a considerable period, for example, in Europe, from the days of the first schools for blind children in the eighteenth century. Its strength as a foundation has been questioned, however.

Three concerns have been voiced about the epistemology or knowledge base of special education. The first is the perceived false legitimacy of special educational knowledge and the need to trust in common sense knowledge and basic humanity. The second concern relates to the quality of special education research and methods of assessment and pedagogy. The third criticism has to do with the role of 'reductionist epistemology', which is a view of knowledge that encourages limited perceptions of individuals in the separation of children (Thomas and Loxley, 2007, especially chapter 2, pp. 22–46). When provided in parenthesis, references to these authors are abbreviated throughout this chapter, for example '(T&L, 2007, pp. 22–46)'.

The present chapter responds to these three concerns. It then points to the wide base of knowledge of foundational disciplines such as sociology, psycholinguistics and neuropsychology. This leads to a brief consideration of the methods of special education and evidence-based practice.

Special education knowledge

Concerns about the perceived scientific orientation of special educational knowledge

Some special education commentators such as Heshusius (1991) take the radical position of seeking to question the foundations of science, as does Lyotard's report for the Quebec government (Lyotard, F. ([1979]/1984). Others accept scientific understanding as it applies to the hard sciences, but question its application to the social fields. In the latter view, special education may be presented as being based on apparently scientific foundations, such as psychology and sociology. These disciplines are taken to inform rational empirically based attempts to understand, explain and support or remedy the difficulties of children who find it hard to learn or behave. It is suggested this knowledge base is only spuriously scientific, being weak in both theory and evidence (T&L, 2007, pp. 22–46).

Special education it is maintained has aggrandized theoretical, empirical and particularly scientific knowledge, which has been projected as consistent and objective. This, it is said, has created misleading credibility for the development of special education and the work of special educators. However, more recently, certainties are being challenged and it is said to be increasingly recognized that there are 'no special means of getting to knowledge about the human world' (T&L, 2007, p. 29).

It is claimed that the successful methods of science leading to progress in the hard sciences such as physics and chemistry, have been too readily assumed to apply to social sciences, such as psychology and sociology. The methods of supposedly scientific psychology and sociology have led to a 'garbled, two dimensional discourse' limiting our basic human recognition of others' difficulties (T&L, 2007, p. 29). Such tenets and methods of psychologists and sociologists have been taken up too eagerly and unquestioningly by those involved in special education. The knowledge produced by the scientific study of psychology and psychiatry, it is stated, has simply supported 'everyday constructions about disability, difference or disorder'.

Some of the ideas of the French historian and philosopher Michel Foucault may help one recognize that social structures, including special schools, and special pedagogy and assessment are not inevitable but stem from people's purposeful action (T&L, 2007, p. 30). It is suggested that special assessment and special pedagogy as constituents of special education create a mistrust of 'common sense knowledge' of pedagogy, leading to teachers losing confidence in their capability to teach and assess all the children with whom they work (T&L, 2007, p. 27).

The argument against the knowledge base of special education then concerns its over-reliance on scientific tenets where they appear to be unjustifiable. So what might be an appropriate response to such concerns?

Responses to criticisms of the perceived overly scientific basis of special education

The knowledge base of special education does not just comprise elements of psychology and sociology, important as these are. It also includes the day-to-day working knowledge of teachers and others in seeing what works and what does not in helping children learn and develop. It is hard to recognze a scenario in which teachers are caught up in some kind of epistemological tsunami that obliterates from their consciousness their everyday interactions with children. Anyone regularly visiting teachers educating special children in mainstream or special school classrooms would find it hard to recognize such a picture. They may instead conclude that teachers are drawing on a range of approaches in a level-headed, sensible way. This is not, of course, common sense knowledge. It is knowledge informed by training and professional development built up over time and refined by day-to-day experience and practice.

Thomas and Loxley (2007) place much confidence in common sense knowledge and see any mistrust of it as a bad thing. But it is, ironically, reliance on apparently common sense views that they say has led to an uncritical acceptance of supposed scientific knowledge. The notion that scientific knowledge was uncritically accepted is suspected of leading to the (as they see it) present unhappy situation.

But teachers are asked to have confidence in their common sense knowledge to challenge orthodoxy, leaving important questions unanswered. Who is to say that the common sense knowledge about teaching and learning is better than any earlier version of common sense knowledge? What happens where teachers and others have differing versions of what constitutes common sense knowledge? They might, of course, meet regularly to do some problem solving so that new approaches could somehow emerge. However, while this is happening, it seems perverse and wasteful not to draw on existing approaches that are seen to work.

Few people would disagree that plenty of common humanity is a good thing. The difference might arise where people have a different idea of how common humanity might be expressed. The teacher and others can encourage '. . . interest, confidence, freedom from worry' and be 'warm and patient' (T&L, 2007, p. 27). All this is compatible with inclusion and with providing a good education. But rather more is needed to ensure a child is learning and developing as well as possible.

Overall, the criticisms that the knowledge base of special education is overly scientific seem ill founded and poorly informed. They fail to take account of the way teachers integrate special educational knowledge with professional judgement and with the knowledge and skills associated with day-to-day teaching. The suggestion that the knowledge base of special education should be replaced by common sense takes too uncritical a view of what common sense might be. While everyone can support the uncontroversial view that there should be more common humanity, it is necessary to specify how this is expressed.

Special education research and interventions

General mistrust of research and interventions in special education

However, concerns are not just restricted to a scientific basis for special educational knowledge. There are also reservations about related research. It is intimated that it is not possible to find in special education any putative advance in 'practice-from-research' in the previous 100 years. Specific research may give rise to beneficial effects in special education practice. But, too often, when the research is later evaluated, its interventions are shown to be only as good as non-research-based methods (T&L, 2007, p. 24). Relatedly, it is suggested, special education has produced numerous methods and techniques claiming some empirical justification. Among those attracting criticism are behavioural psychology and direct instruction (ibid. p. 25). The remainder of the present section examines the criticisms and the extent to which they are justified.

In considering the extent of the usefulness of research in special education, Thomas and Loxley (2007, p. 38) recognize an obvious criticism of their views. This is that they point out supposed flaws in research in special education, yet accept evidence on school outcome research when it seems to support their case. One minute they are decrying special education research for being spurious, the next they are quoting it to try to demonstrate outcomes are poor. One the one hand, they maintain that regarding research into people and their social environments it is barely possible to 'delineate variables for inspection of their effects' (ibid. p. 25). On the other hand, they are eager to quote research that purportedly shows approaches in a negative light.

Undoubtedly, in some cases, new methods do little more, when carefully evaluated, than ordinary approaches or already used approaches that may be simpler and cheaper. But where new methods are found, providing they are not overly complicated or inordinately expensive, they may be welcome. At the very least, they may provide an alternative approach that is just as good as other methods.

But even more than this, research and supposed 'treatments' in special education have sometimes been misguided. This may be due to several reasons. Schools and parents may be too eager to find approaches appearing to promise great progress so that they do not always scrutinize claims rigorously enough. Charismatic proponents of new methods may carry people along with their enthusiasm, which might later prove ill founded. Commercial interests may play their part in exaggerating reasonable claims. Examples of such 'fad' approaches have been well illustrated (Hornby *et al.*, 1997).

For example, in a chapter, 'Facilitated communication – fact or fantasy?' Hornby and colleagues examine claims for this intervention (Hornby *et al.*, 1997, pp. 157–166). Facilitated communication was a method of helping non-verbal individuals to communicate using a keyboard or by pointing to alphabet letters on a board. A facilitator guided the child's arm, hand or finger to press keys or point to letters. It was used with children with physical impairment, moderate to severe cognitive impairment and autism (Bebko *et al.*, 1996, p. 20). After reviewing the evidence, Hornby and colleagues conclude, 'there is no reliable support for the validity of FC' and 'there is a large amount of evidence indicating that the source of the communications produced is the facilitators themselves' (Hornby *et al.*, 1997, p. 165).

But Thomas and Loxley (2007) go beyond pointing to interventions that have been shown to be limited or invalid. They give a few examples of what they take to be controversial approaches and generalize from these that special education research and special education approaches overall are questionable and too much in the grip of scientific aspirations. Yet even the examples they offer to demonstrate their critical views are open to more positive interpretations. Consider direct instruction and the broader area of behavioural psychology.

Direct instruction

Direct instruction involves teaching and learning formal skills and clearly specifying content, method and evaluation. It involves regular assessment. Originally developed by Engelmann and Becker at the University of Oregon in the 1960s, it was the focus of a federally funded programme called Project Follow Through. However, a study by Schweinhart and Welkhart (1997), according to Thomas and Loxley (2007, p. 26) found that children who took part in Direct Instruction were 'significantly more likely' on leaving school when they were older to be 'involved in crime'.

It is not explained what the purported link between being taught skills formally and committing crime might be. It is acknowledged that Direct Instruction can lead to 'great benefits', but it is suggested these may be as much to do with generous funding as to particular aspects of pedagogy (T&L, 2007, p. 26). This does not seem to be much of a criticism. Unless the suggestion that Direct Instruction is related in some systematic way to a later criminal career can be demonstrated, the approach seems to have something going for it.

In fact, studies with negative findings (e.g. Ryder, Burton and Silberg, 2006) are fairly isolated. High gains in achievement have been reported using Direct Instruction (Rebar, 2007). Considering 25 investigations in which Direct Instruction was compared with other interventions, White (1988) found that none of the studies showed results favouring the comparison groups. Some 53% of the outcomes significantly favoured Direct Instruction with a (large) average effect size of 0.84. Adams and Engelmann (1996) analysed 37 research studies involving Direct Instruction programmes compared with other interventions. Studies involving a total of 21 special education students were analysed separately, showing a (large) mean effect size of 0.90. Forness *et al.* (1997) found strong evidence of the success of Direct Instruction for students receiving special education services. The Comprehensive School Reform quality centre site shows Direct Instruction to be one of the most effective models of comprehensive school reform. Please see (www.csrq.org/ CSRQreportselementaryschoolreport.asp) (See also Carnine *et al.*, 2004).

Behavioural psychology

It is suggested that, for children with severe learning difficulties, there is an 'overuse of the technology of behavioural psychology' (T&L, 2007, p. 25). (In the English classification system, 'severe learning difficulties' is broadly parallel with what in the United States of America is referred to as 'moderate to severe mental retardation' or in some other countries, 'moderate to severe cognitive impairment'.) Behavioural techniques were used to help learning and encourage appropriate behaviour. It is maintained they may have 'provided some assistance in thinking about pedagogy for some children', but they oversimplified the nature of learning and tended to lead to a rather barren curriculum (ibid. p. 25).

It is fair to note that behavioural approaches can lead to rather barren curricula if they are overused. However, the *over*-use of anything for anyone is, by definition, a bad thing. The question surely is whether the *use* of behavioural psychology can benefit special children. Approaches derived from behavioural psychology have been shown to be effective in modifying children's behaviour and in assisting their learning. Such a wide and well-established research base supports this, that positive reviews and evaluations done decades ago tend to stand. A few examples may illustrate.

In relation to improving behaviour, including that of pupils with behaviour disorders, there is a range of evidence of the effectiveness of behavioural techniques. Classroom group contingencies, that is, rewards and sanctions applied to groups, not just individuals, were analysed by Litow and Pumroy (1975). O'Leary and Drabman (1971) reviewed token economies in the classroom. The use of 'response cost' (losing anticipated rewards because of unwanted behaviour) in school settings was considered by Walker (1983).

Rutherford and Polsgrove (1981) reviewed the use of behaviour contracts with 'behaviourally disordered and delinquent' children and young people. Rutherford and Nelson (1982) examined the literature on the use of time out for 'behaviourally disordered' pupils in classrooms. It has also been demonstrated that, for attention deficit hyperactivity disorder, where medication is taken, behavioural methods can enable the dose to be reduced while maintaining similar improvements in classroom performance (Carlson *et al.*, 1992).

In the area of anxiety disorder, behavioural interventions have been employed effectively in relation to elective mutism, school refusal and phobias. Elective mutism responds to family-based behavioural treatment. This involves the carer attending school with the child and gradually withdrawing over a period of perhaps several weeks (Carr, 2006, p. 251). Behavioural interventions can be effective for many phobic children (Ollendick and King, 1998 provide a review). In one study, mainly of school refusers of secondary school age, behavioural intervention led to significantly better rates of maintenance in school than home tutoring or inpatient treatment (Blagg and Yule, 1984). Contingency management has been demonstrated to be effective with young children with phobias (Menzies and Clarke, 1993).

Pivotal response training uses a model of Applied Behaviour Analysis involving positive child-centred and family-centred procedures. It is intended to improve the social, emotional and communicative behaviour of young children with autistic spectrum disorders (Koegel and Koegel, 1995). A review concludes it is an effective intervention (Humphries, 2003, p. 5). (See also www.researchintopractice.info.) Schedules of differential reinforcement in relation to a person's degree of cognitive impairment have also been examined (Whittaker, 1996).

Numerous examples of the effectiveness of behavioural approaches may be found in Kazdin (2001), Alberto and Troutman (2005) and Pierce and Cheney (2008). This is an impressive track record for a range of approaches that have been described (T&L, 2007, p. 25) as merely having 'provided some assistance in thinking about pedagogy for some children'.

Reductionist epistemology in the separation of children

It has been claimed that, in the early 1900s, a collection of ill-founded and prejudicial ideas were current, including that certain children should be educated separately from the majority. Being associated with philosophy and science legitimized these 'simple notions'. The philosophy of Nietzsche and the science of Darwin were, it is said, 'distorted and misused' and the new technologies of psychology, especially psychometrics, buttressed the developing epistemology. It is suggested that, in the 1940s, views concerning special school effectiveness were predominantly built on ideas of the importance of nature over nurture. Special schools were considered suitable for accommodating some children, while simultaneously protecting the efficient education of most children in mainstream. Furthermore, this 'common sense view' was built on the notion of 'inherited and immutable intelligence' (T&L, 2007, pp. 36–38).

These views, it is said, were not seriously challenged until the 1960s. Following civil rights developments about race in the United States of America, changing perceptions led to questioning what seemed to be 'segregation by ability and disability rather than race' (T&L, 2007, p. 37). Yet the new dominant disciplines of psychology and sociology, along with psychoanalysis, psychiatric social work and educational psychology, have, it is argued, exerted too much influence on special education. The related epistemology has reinforced a taken for granted everyday knowledge that should be challenged. The reductionist direction of special education research has led society not to seek to include children but to 'analyse and fix' (ibid. p. 43).

Thomas and Loxley (2007, pp. 36–38, 42–43) give a version of a perceived historical trend in special education. However, their concentration on the role of supposed 'inherited and immutable' intelligence does not quite explain the development of special provision for children with speech and language impairments, visual impairment, hearing impairments, deafblindness, anxiety disorders, depressive disorders, conduct disorder, autism, orthopaedic impairments or health impairments.

Neither does the potted history reflect any knowledge of the extensive use of intelligence tests in modern day assessment. The *Diagnostic and Statistical Manual of Mental Disorders Fourth Edition Text Revision (DSM-IV-TR)* (American Psychiatric Association, 2000, e.g. p. 42) provides diagnostic criteria for mild, severe, moderate and profound 'mental retardation'. While the criteria include IQ ranges, the guidance stresses repeatedly that these are not the sole criterion. There must also be 'co-current deficits or impairments in present adaptive functioning' in at least two areas from: communication, self care, home living, social/interpersonal skills, use of community resources, self-direction, functional academic skills, work, leisure, health and safety' (ibid.). (Please also see the chapter on 'Assessment' in the present volume.)

Furthermore, other versions of special education history give a quite different picture. For example, Pritchard (1963, p. 1) points out that special educational developments are sometimes seen as running beside progress in scientific endeavours. One of the reasons why special schools were thought to lag behind schools for other children was that specialist techniques were necessary, but were not developed in the early days of special education. Some of them awaited 'advances in science, medicine and mental measurement'. Special schools are seen as the way forward (ibid.).

Cole (1989) sees the 'integration–segregation' questions as a false dichotomy. The concept of integration in his view informed the nineteenth-century pioneers. He observes, 'If there is a clear lesson from history, it is that timeless questions such as whether one should take the special child to the expert, or the expert to the special child, or whether it is better to be normal in an abnormal special school or abnormal in an ordinary school, cannot be answered as dogmatically as many have wished' (ibid. p. 175).

If someone began from a position of despising special schools and mistrusting special education and wanting to degrade it, one could perhaps understand how a selective gloss on history could be concocted to support this. But historical research is not an area where one can be over-selective with evidence. Where there are different interpretations of evidence, there surely needs to be some recognition of evidence that runs counter to one's hypotheses. A potted history that gives a completely malign picture of psychology and sociology and depicts psychometrics as little better than eugenics is unlikely to be very convincing, certainly not to historians, still less to psychologists and sociologists.

Foundational disciplines of special education

So far, the chapter has considered only a limited knowledge base relating to special education in order to address particular criticisms. However, the knowledge base of special education is much wider than this. Special education draws on a range of foundational disciplines and knowledge. These contribute to the understanding and practice of special education and to provision for different types of disability and disorder.

Examining the perceived epistemology of special education is itself part of the philosophical knowledge base in that it seeks to clarify what is known and what can be known in the area. Other aspects of philosophy such as the careful analysis of concepts can help clarify and question some of the assumptions made and the views taken in special education.

Special education also draws on other disciplines such as medicine (including psychiatry), neuropsychology and psychotherapy (especially behavioural, systemic and psychodynamic approaches). Further disciplines are sociology, behavioural psychology, child development and observational learning in social learning theory. Others are pedagogy to the extent that this seeks to apply knowledge from many sources to learning, and psycholinguistics. Legal frameworks and classifications of disability and disorder influence the contours of special education. Technology makes another important contribution (Farrell, 2009a).

Some foundations have relevance for several types of disability and disorder, as with 'developmental' considerations, which can inform for example understandings of reading disorder and developmental coordination disorder. Provision for some types of disability or disorder may be informed by several foundational disciplines, as with provision for profound cognitive impairment, which can draw on developmental perspectives, medicine, technological considerations and others.

Many of these disciplines seek to be scientific in their approach, commensurate with the fact that they are involved in the complexity of human behaviour and thought. There is a risk of placing too much faith in the findings and tenets of these disciplines. Certainly, information and understanding drawn from these areas needs to be tempered with professional knowledge and insight into children and their families. Any legitimacy that special education has needs to be informed by humility about the complexity of the challenges that face families, teachers and others when seeking the best provision for special children.

Methods of special education

Many currently used methods, such as behavioural strategies for children with conduct disorder, are intended to aid the learning and development of special children. These are kept under review to ensure they continue to provide the anticipated benefits. Newer, promising methods can be analysed to identify their important and effective elements and to try to establish why they work. Attempts are made to generalize from particular examples to wider applications and from a few pupils to many. Hypotheses relating to such findings may be tested and evaluated, contributing to evidence-based practice. Methodology therefore ranges from observation and description used for critical reflection, to hypotheses and theory.

An enactment of the No Child Left Behind Act 2002 in the United States of America is relevant here. The Act provides that all students, including those with disabilities, will demonstrate annual yearly progress and perform at a proficient level on state academic assessment tests. Identifying scientific methods and evidence-based practices can contribute to this aspiration, but is challenging. Relatedly, Simpson (2005), considering autism, makes observations with wider relevance.

Evidence will involve peer review. Ideally, products and materials would be validated through research designs using random samples and control and experimental groups. However, other methods such as single subject design validation or correlational methods may be acceptable in some circumstances. There may be a limited sample of pupils, and the researcher may need to be flexible in matching research designs to particular issues (Simpson, 2005, p. 142, paraphrased). Parents and professionals should know about the efficacy and anticipated outcomes for interventions. They will need to know the most effective means of evaluation, potential risks, and whether anticipated outcomes are in line with the child's needs (p. 143, paraphrased). Evidence-based practice can inform decisions, but these are also influenced by professional judgement and by the views of the child and family.

Conclusion

The notion that a falsely legitimized scientifically constrained knowledge typifies special education overlooks the breadth of the knowledge base and the role of the day-to-day professional working knowledge of teachers. The alternative of trusting common sense knowledge faces the difficulty of agreeing what common sense is for different individuals. Extolling common humanity is uncontentious, but there are different views about how it might be expressed.

Denying the validity of special education research cannot be justified unless all social research is rejected, including that purporting to support inclusion. Selective readings of the history of special education can be used either to support or criticize separate provision for special children. Foundational disciplines of special education provide a wide and comprehensive source of relevant knowledge. The importance of methods supporting evidence-based practice are recognized in legislation and in professional practice.

Summary statement: knowledge base

The knowledge base of special education includes a wide range of disciplines and contributions supplemented by related research and methods informing evidence-based practice. It is tempered by training and professional judgement about what works in day-to-day teaching.

Thinking points

Readers may wish to consider:

- what might be considered part of the knowledge base of special education;
- the status of special education research and related interventions;
- the historical background to the development of special schools.

Further reading

Hornby, G., Atkinson, M. and Howard, J. (1997) *Controversial Issues in Special Education*. London, David Fulton.

This book robustly examines controversial areas in special education. These are diagnoses (autism, dyslexia, attention deficit hyperactivity disorder); system-wide interventions (integration and exclusions); group interventions (conductive education, instrumental enrichment, peer/parent tutoring); and individual interventions (coloured lenses and overlays, facilitated communication and reading recovery).

Other key texts

Alberto, P. A. and Troutman, A. C. (2005) (7th edition) *Applied Behavioural Analysis for Teachers*. Columbus, OH, Merrill/Prentice Hall.

A practically orientated book covering the concepts and techniques of behaviour management. It includes: identifying the target behaviour, collecting and presenting behaviour data, functional assessment, experimental design, arranging antecedents and consequences, generalizing changes in behaviour and ethical issues.

Thomas, G. and Loxley, A. (2007) (2nd edition) *Deconstructing Special Education and Constructing Inclusion*. Maidenhead, United Kingdom, Open University Press/McGraw-Hill.

This book provides some criticisms of special education and proposes more inclusive education and schools in its place. 'The knowledge roots of special education' is chapter 2 of the book.

Chapter 6

The unhelpfulness of classifications

This chapter considers the nature of classification. It describes categorical classifications of disabilities and disorders such as 'developmental coordination disorder' and 'reading disorder' used in the United States of America and in England. The chapter presents various criticisms of the use of categorical classification in attempting to delineate disabilities and disorders, and outlines possible responses. A different, dimensional system of classification is examined. Possible productive relationships between dimensional and categorical classifications are suggested.

What is classification?

Classifications can be made of many phenomena. Data on a local population might be gathered and used by a local authority to plan health, education, leisure and other services and facilities. Among the information a local authority might wish to know is the different age groups within the population. They might want to establish how many of the population are aged 0 to 5 years, 18 to 25 years, over 70 years old and so on.

Identification involves making operational the definitions that have emerged from the classification (for example, children aged 0 to 5 years). Having decided on these defining qualities, individual members of the population can be identified and allocated to one of the categories.

Assessment of an individual could involve applying the operational definition or several operational definitions to a person. Consequently, one person might be aged 18 to 25, be male, and be educated to university graduate level. Classifications of people might involve the defining attributes of sex, age, educational level, or other characteristics.

It will be seen that some of the classifications involve discrete entities such as sex so that the classification is that someone is male or female. Other classifications concern phenomena that are continuously distributed such as age, where some kind of judgement is made about cut-off points for different purposes such as under 5 years old, or 11 to 16 years old. Where continuously distributed characteristics are classified, there is usually some explanation of the various cut-off points. For example, if one is looking at leisure provision, the habits of leisure use might be expected to be different at different life periods, justifying gathering and grouping data according to certain age ranges.

A good system of classification allows predictions to be made about others who were not in the original sample. It may be found from a sample that the sporting and leisure pursuits of individuals aged 60 to 70 differed from those of individuals aged 20 to 30 in systematic ways; for example, the preference for golf over squash among older people. If the age classifications have been well chosen, then it is more likely that such preferences would be found if further people in the two age groups were questioned.

In more general terms, classifications therefore involve several features. They imply deciding upon a set of defining qualities or attributes. From a larger group, smaller groups are differentiated according to the extent to which they relate to the defined qualities. These smaller groups are coherent and more homogenous than the original larger group.

Identification involves individuals being allocated to a subgroup constituting the classification. It represents making operational the definitions that arise from the classification. Assessment is the process of applying the operational definitions to individuals to decide membership in one or several partitions.

Good classifications are reliable in the sense that they are not dependent on the method of classification and 'replicate in other samples'. Also, they have sufficient coverage allowing suitable identification; and help communication and prediction (Fletcher *et al.*, 2003 pp. 34–35, paraphrased).

Classifications of disabilities and disorders

Classifications of disabilities and disorders are used in many countries. These classifications relate to conceptions of typical development, syndromes, or injury affecting several areas of development, the functioning of sensory faculties, and the supposed effects of brain processing.

In the United States of America, pupils considered to need special education covered by federal law have a defined disability, and the disability has an adverse educational impact. Categories of disability under federal law as amended in 1997 (20 United States Code 1402, 1997) are reflected in subsequent 'designated disability codes' as follows:

01   mentally retarded
02   hard-of-hearing
03   deaf
04   speech and language impaired
05   visually handicapped
06   emotionally disturbed
07   orthopaedically impaired
08   other health impaired
09   specific learning disability

10   multi-handicapped
11   child in need of assessment
12   deafblind
13   traumatic brain injury
14   autism.

In England, a similar classification (Department for Education and Skills, 2005, passim) comprises:

- specific learning difficulties (e.g. dyslexia, dyscalculia, dyspraxia)
- learning difficulty (moderate, severe, profound)
- behavioural, emotional and social difficulty
- speech, language and communication needs
- autistic spectrum disorder
- visual impairment
- hearing impairment
- multi-sensory impairment
- physical disability.

In the American system, mild, severe to moderate, and profound mental retardation is similar to the English classification of moderate, severe and profound learning difficulties (Farrell, 2001, pp. 1–5).

A slightly more detailed classification may be used drawing on those used in the systems in the United States of America and in England, those used in the *Diagnostic and Statistical Manual of Mental Disorders Fourth Edition Text Revision* (*DSM-IV-TR*) (American Psychiatric Association, 2000), and speech and language pathology distinctions (see also Farrell, 2008a, pp. 3–6). This aims to make it possible to draw on research and professional opinion concerning therapy and related educational initiatives that use similar distinctions. The suggested classifications are as follows:

- profound cognitive impairment (compares with 'profound learning difficulty' and 'profound mental retardation');
- moderate to severe cognitive impairment (compares with 'severe learning difficulty' and 'moderate to severe mental retardation');
- mild cognitive impairment (compares with 'moderate learning difficulty' and 'mild mentally retardation');
- hearing impairment (compares with 'hard-of-hearing/deaf');
- visual impairment (compares with 'visually handicapped');
- deafblindness (compares with 'multi-sensory impairment');
- orthopaedic impairment and motor disorder (compares with 'physical disability' and 'orthopaedically impaired');
- health impairment (compares with 'physical disability' and 'other health impaired');
- traumatic brain injury;

- disruptive behaviour disorders including conduct disorder (compares with 'behavioural, emotional and social difficulty' and 'emotionally disturbed');
- anxiety disorders and depressive disorders (compares with 'behavioural, emotional and social difficulty' and 'emotionally disturbed');
- attention deficit hyperactivity disorder (compares with 'behavioural, emotional and social difficulty' and 'other health impaired');
- communication disorders – speech (compares with 'speech, language and communication needs' and 'speech and language impaired');
- communication disorders – grammar, comprehension (compares with 'speech, language and communication needs' and 'speech and language impaired');
- communication disorders – semantics, pragmatics (compares with 'speech, language and communication needs' and 'speech and language impaired');
- autism (compares with 'autistic spectrum disorder/autism');
- developmental co-ordination disorder (compares with 'specific learning difficulties (dyspraxia)' and 'specific learning disability (developmental coordination disorder)';
- reading disorder (compares with 'specific learning difficulties – dyslexia' and 'specific learning disability – reading disorder)';
- disorder of written expression (compares with 'specific learning difficulties', often as an aspect of dyslexia, and 'specific learning disability – disorder of written expression';
- mathematics disorder (compares with 'specific learning difficulties – dyscalculia' and 'specific learning disability – mathematics disorder').

Challenges to categorical classification and responses

There are several criticisms of categorical classification. These criticisms and possible responses are considered below.

Continuously distributed characteristics and classifications

Some classifications are questioned where they involve attempting to compartmentalise continuously distributed characteristics. It was mentioned earlier that, when continuously distributed characteristics such as age, or height or weight are categorized, some kind of judgement is made about cut-off points and some explanation is offered about the divisions. For example, categorizing by weight including the categorical classifications, 'under-weight', 'normal range', 'over-weight' and 'obese' might be justified by a local health service to identify people at risk of heart conditions.

Issues of trying to classify continuously distributed characteristics arise with regard to disabilities and disorders. Intelligence is considered a continuously distributed characteristic. Scores of individuals on intelligence tests are continuously distributed from individuals who score very highly to those whose scores are very low. If one is going to propose broad classifications of these scores, it is helpful to explain why.

In relation to the broad divisions of intelligence test scores that contribute to assessments of different degrees of cognitive impairment, the justification is that children may need different kinds of provision within certain ranges of cognitive impairment as partly reflected by the range of scores. For example, a child with profound cognitive impairment may require greater support and education helping him make full use of his senses and integrate them. At the same time, intelligence test scores are not used as the sole criterion for assessment and functional skills are also assessed (American Psychiatric Association, 2000, pp. 41–42).

Categories may militate against seeing the child holistically

There is a concern that, where categories of disability or disorder are used, they can obscure the fact that parents, teachers and others are interacting with a child not a condition. This may be a factor leading to care with language such as the 'person first' suggestion that one might refer to 'a child with autism' in preference to 'an autistic child'. Responses to such suggestions depend on one's views of whether language predominantly shapes perception or whether the use of language reflects perceptions of social and material reality. In the light of this, such suggestions are either considered to reflect sensitivity or to be mere political correctness.

Nevertheless, terminology is argued to be a factor in shaping personal identity. The way one refers to oneself and the way others see one clearly have some influence on shaping identity in potentially positive and negative ways. Certainly, parents and professionals need to remain aware that categories are concerned with delineating disabilities and disorders, not children. Care is needed that classification of a disorder or disability does not come to be seen as a classification of the child.

It is also relevant that categories are used as temporary viewpoints from which some factors may be seen that may otherwise be missed. For example, if a child is identified as having developmental coordination disorder, a whole range of behaviours misperceived by parents and teachers may fall into place. The pupil who is late for lessons may not be uncooperative but may have needed longer to attend to toileting demands at recess time and have taken longer to find the classroom in large busy high school/secondary school. The fact that he then enters the room and bumps into other pupils and trips over bags may not be seen by the teacher as adding insult to injury to disturb the lesson. It may be recognized that he genuinely may not be able to negotiate such obstacles easily.

Wide variations in the apparent prevalence of disabilities and disorders

The validity and reliability of some categories of disability and disorder may be questioned. If a category is clear and well defined, one expectation is that there would be a considerable degree of agreement how many children are identified in different localities and by different people. These would be expected to be similar unless there were reasons to assume otherwise.

Yet, sometimes there are very wide variations in the supposed prevalence of conditions.

Examples are oppositional defiant disorder and conduct disorder (American Psychiatric Association, 2000). In the criteria of the *DSM-IV-TR* (American Psychiatric Association, 2000) the essential feature of oppositional defiant disorder is a repeated pattern (lasting at least for 6 months) of behaviour towards people in authority that is, 'negativistic, defiant, disobedient, and hostile' (ibid. p. 100). The behaviour leads to significant impairment in 'social, academic or occupational functioning' (p. 100).

The prevalence of oppositional defiant disorder varies from 2% to 16%. Such a wide variation cannot inspire confidence that what is being identified and classified is very valid or that the assessment is reliable. The variation depends on the nature of the population sample and the methods of assessment. It may also relate to the difficulty of determining whether apparent oppositional defiant disorder is a justifiable category or whether the behaviour if it occurs in school arises predominantly from poor teaching and inadequate behaviour management.

Similarly, the prevalence of conduct disorder varies considerably. In the general population reported rates range from 1% to 10% (American Psychiatric Association, 2000, p. 97). The variations relate to the nature of the population sampled and on the methods used to ascertain conduct disorder. Nevertheless, such differences suggest a certain caution is appropriate when using the category.

Co-occurrence and inferences about provision

Issues of category boundaries also arise in relation to the co-occurrence of various disorders and disabilities. Around half of clinic-referred children with attention deficit hyperactivity disorder also have oppositional defiant disorder or conduct disorder (American Psychiatric Association, 2000, p. 88). This may reflect conceptual overlap or possible underlying factors that predispose a child to several disorders and may ultimately lead in the future to the use of a newly developed category.

Also, disorder of written expression and mathematics disorder are often associated with reading disorder. In fact, it is relatively unusual for either to be present in the absence of reading disorder (American Psychiatric Association, 2000, p. 52). Language deficits and perceptual motor deficits may accompany disorder of written expression (ibid. p. 55). Indeed, the co-occurrence of various disabilities and disorders may reflect common underlying difficulties as suggested in legislative definitions of 'learning disability' in the United States of America's classification system.

Such co-occurrence leads to questions about the validity of categories, and whether broader or different categories might be more accurate and useful. But they also have implications for attempts to relate types of disability and disorder to distinctive profiles of provision, where it is claimed that particular types of disabilities and disorders suggest certain types of provision.

Reading disorder may suggest speech-language therapy, work on phonics and related interventions to compensate for phonological deficit (Farrell, 2008a, chapter 19). With regard to developmental coordination disorder, approaches include the use of adapted equipment for domestic tasks, extra time for routines such as changing clothes for physical education and careful training to support handwriting (ibid. chapter 18). For mathematics disorder, there may be an emphasis on establishing pre-requisite skills such as classification, reducing any anxiety associated with mathematics and providing many concrete examples (ibid. chapter 21).

Where reading disorder, mathematics disorder and developmental disorder co-occur, the implications for provision may not appear as clear as when they are consider separately. In fact, practical considerations can point the way to suitable compromises. Mathematics disorder may be related to issues associated with reading disorder such as visual processing difficulties. Similarly, mathematics difficulties might be related to the difficulties associated with developmental coordination disorder such as problems with aligning numbers. The approaches to provision in such instances will be those suitable for reading disorder or developmental coordination disorder but adapted for mathematics disorder (Farrell, 2008a, chapter 21).

Wider categories and unitary syndromes

There is also debate about the extent to which groups of disorders and disabilities might be meaningfully considered as a wider category or unitary syndrome. Learning disability, under the United States of America, *Individuals with Disabilities Act* is, '. . . a disorder in one or more basic psychological processes involved in understanding or in using language, spoken or written, that may manifest itself in an imperfect ability to listen, think, speak, read, write, spell, or to do mathematical calculations . . .' (34 C. F. R. section 300.7 (b) (10)).

Despite appropriate learning experiences being provided, the child does not achieve 'commensurate with his or her age and ability levels in one or more of the areas listed' and there is a 'severe discrepancy' between achievement and intellectual ability in one or more of the specified areas (oral expression, listening comprehension, written expression, basic reading skill, reading comprehension, mathematics calculation or mathematics reasoning) (34 C. F. R. section 300.541 (a)).

More briefly, learning disability has been described as, 'a heterogeneous set of disorders that include difficulty (not predicted from measures of general cognitive aptitude) in a variety of cognitive and social domains' (Cutting and Denckla, 2003, p. 125). In fact, a reauthorization of the *Individuals with Disabilities Act* (House Bill 1350) in 2004 removed the requirement that schools show that students identified as having a learning disability have discrepant ability and achievement. The *Individuals with Disabilities Act* definition excludes factors that might be expected to contribute to lower achievement, such as 'mental retardation' or 'emotional disturbance' (Lyon *et al.*, 2001).

Similarly, there is debate about the extent to which developmental coordination disorder; specific developmental disorder of motor function (*ICD-10*, World Health Organization, 1992); and developmental dyslexia can be considered a unitary syndrome with regard to symptoms, aetiology, treatment response and outcome

(Cantell *et al.*, 2001). There is the possibility that some categories may be reshaped as evidence from newer sources such as neuropsychology are brought to bear.

General points

Many of the classifications used in relation to special education are part of the *Diagnostic and Statistical Manual of Mental Disorders Fourth Edition Text Revision (DSM-IV-TR)*. This is a categorical classification that divides mental disorders into types 'based on criteria sets with defining features' (ibid. p. xxxi). The editors of *DSM-IV-TR* (American Psychiatric Association, 2000) note, 'The need for a classification of mental disorders has been clear throughout the history of medicine' (p. xxiv). They accept that care is needed when using categories. Furthermore, they do not assume each category is a 'completely discrete entity' with 'absolute' boundaries that divide it from other mental disorders or from no mental disorder (p. xxxi).

Professional judgement is also needed. The editors recognize the range and differences of clinical presentation. Consequently, *DSM-IV* often includes 'polythetic criteria sets' in which the individual is diagnosed using only a subset of items from a fuller list. It is recognized there is debate about which disorders should be included and the optimal method of their organization (American Psychiatric Association, 2000, p. xxxii).

Dimensional classification

The International Classification of Functioning, Disability and Health

It is sometimes suggested that dimensional systems of classifying health and capacity such as those developed by the World Health Organization (2002, 2007) are more justifiable than categorical classifications such as 'conduct disorder' (American Psychiatric Association, 2000).

The *International Classification of Functioning, Disability and Health* (*ICF*) (World Health Organization, 2002) is a classification system concentrating on individual functional difference across several areas. It also seeks to recognize biological, psychological and social factors relevant to functioning. In the *ICF*, disability covers impairments, participation restrictions and activity limitations. Disability is seen as an interaction of: bodily functions and structures, activities and participation in one's present environment.

These dimensions are influenced by both health conditions and by contextual factors. *ICF* identifies an individual in terms of body function; body structure; activity and participation; and contextual factors. Using a similar model and assumptions, the *International Classification of Functioning, Disability and Health: Children and Youth Version* or *ICF-CY* (World Health Organization, 2007) covers ages from birth to 18 years. Being multidimensional, and focusing on activities and participation, is intended to allow it to monitor change through the life span.

One-level and two-level classification

The 'one-level' classification comprises: body functions, body structures, activities and participation and environmental factors.

Body functions include, for example, mental functions; sensory functions; voice and speech functions; and neuromusculoskeletal and movement related functions (World Health Organization, 2007, pp. 45–105). Body structures generally concern those relating to the bodily functions such as the structures of the nervous system (pp. 107–127).

Activities and participation consists of: learning and applying knowledge; general tasks and demands; communication; mobility; self-care; domestic life; interpersonal interactions and relationships; major life areas; and community, social and civic life (pp. 129–188).

Environmental factors are: products and technology; natural environment and human-made changes to the environment; support and relationships; attitudes; and services, systems and policies (pp. 189–223).

Each of these is further subdivided in a two-level classification. For example, under body functions – mental functions, these consist of 'global mental functions' and 'specific mental functions'. Under body structures – the eye, ear and related structures, are 'structure of the eye socket', 'structure of the eyeball', 'structure of the inner ear' and others. Within activities and participation – self-care, is 'washing oneself', 'caring for body parts', 'toileting' and so on. Within environmental factors – support and relationships include 'immediate family' and 'strangers'.

Aspects of dimensional classification

It is said that a dimensional model, can beneficially shift the unit of classification from diagnosis to the functional characteristics of the child, in keeping with a 'holistic and non- stigmatizing' approach to disability (Simeonson et al., 2008, p. 217). This assumes that non-dimensional disability classifications are inevitably fragmentary and stigmatizing.

It is suggested the ICF might be used to construct a classification of educational disability with greater relevance to 'curriculum and teaching decisions and practices'. However, it is recognized that currently ICF-CY, '... may not have specific relevance to educational provision, defined in curriculum and pedagogic terms' (Norwich, 2008, p. 147). In the context of present non-dimensional classifications such as 'autism', a dimensional approach might enable descriptions of functioning, monitoring of progress and the provision of resources.

In a dimensional classification, individual children with different categorical disabilities or disorders may share similar functional profiles having implications for resources and service delivery. A child with 'traumatic brain injury' and one with 'learning disabilities' may have similar profiles of functional limitation in attending, recalling, and carrying out academic tasks (Simeonson et al., 2008, p. 218).

However, categorical classifications can provide information and possible prognoses that dimensional approaches may not. Medical, social, behavioural, psychological, personal, physical and other implications commonly associated with traumatic brain injury are well documented (Schoenbrodt, 2001). In the *Diagnostic and Statistical Manual of Mental Disorders Fourth Edition Text Revision* (American Psychiatric Association, 2000), dimensional models are rejected. This is partly because they are considered to have been less useful in clinical practice and in stimulating research. Also, numerical dimensional systems are less familiar than the categorical names for mental disorders (ibid. p. xxxii).

Benefits of classification

Important in response to such debates are principles of classification (Fletcher *et al.*, 2003, pp. 34–35). The validity and reliability of categories can be tested, leading to clearer and more robust categories. For classification to be useful, terminology has to be as clear as possible. But equally important is the relationship between constructs and forms of assessment, and between assessment and interventions (Larkin and Cermac, 2002, p. 90). It is also possible that future research, for example, in genetics, brain imaging and neuroscience may lead to a reshaping of some of the categories presently used.

Despite the challenges of delineating such disorders, it can be argued that much that is useful to teachers and others can be identified in research and professional practice referring to categorical classifications to provide for children with such disorders. This includes useful practical implications for provision and prognosis (Fletcher *et al.*, 1999).

Categorical classification allows generalizations to be made about the disorder or disability that can contribute to evidence-based practice. In this respect, 'conduct disorder', 'anxiety disorders' and 'depressive disorders' are clearer than the amorphous term 'emotional, behavioural and social difficulties'.

One of the benefits of suitable classification is that it can have useful practical implications. For example, identifying learning disability or attention deficit hyperactivity disorder (or learning disability and attention deficit hyperactivity disorder occurring together) has implications for provision (academic remediation, behaviour modification and medication), and the prognosis (Fletcher *et al.*, 1999).

Attempts have been made to indicate profiles of distinctive provision for different types of disability and disorder (Farrell, 2008, passim). Provision is seen in terms of the curriculum and assessment, pedagogy, resources, school and classroom organization, and therapy. This distinctive provision is set in the context of provision that responds to the learning and development of all children and is common to all. It also rests in the context of provision that is suitable for a child as an individual that is not shared by others. Nevertheless, it is argued that there is also provision that is suitable by virtue of being relevant to particular types of disability or disorder. In the present text, the chapter on 'Special provision' summarizes some of the approaches that are distinctive for different types of disability and disorder.

Conclusion

Classification appears to be a necessary aspect of special education. With regard to categorical classifications, it is essential to remember that the disorder or disability, not the child, is being categorized. Also, care is necessary that using a category does not detract from seeing the whole child. For some types of disability and disorder, certain factors reduce the confidence that can be placed in categories. One of these factors, the wide ranges of supposed prevalence, can be regarded as a practical issue where discussion between professionals, parents, and administrators can lead to better agreement about criteria and more reliable application of them. Another factor, the co-occurrence of some disabilities and disorders, may reflect several common underpinning processes. This may lead in time to other categories that maintain helpful links between the category and effective provision. There is some movement in this direction indicated by the broad categorization of 'learning disabilities' in the United States of America.

There are some strengths in the use of non-categorical, dimensional classifications, although these too have their weaknesses. Among the strongest benefits of categorical classification are opportunities to establish evidence-related provision. Additionally, dimensional classification might be used for monitoring the progress of individuals and groups and to inform the allocation of resources.

Summary statement

Categorical classifications such as 'autism' or 'profound cognitive impairment' can support evidence related provision, and dimensional classifications such as 'participation restrictions' and 'activity limitations' can enable monitoring of progress of individuals and groups, and inform resource allocation.

Thinking points

Readers may wish to consider:

- the relative merits of a dimensional approach and a categorical approach to classification;
- the extent to which dimensional and categorical classifications can be compatible in rationale and in practical use.

Key text

American Psychiatric Association (2000) *Diagnostic and Statistical Manual of Mental Disorders Fourth Edition Text Revision.* Washington DC, APA.

This provides classificatory criteria for identifying many disorders and disabilities, as well as a rationale for this approach. It includes diagnostic criteria for a range of disorders. These include: mild, moderate, severe and profound cognitive impairment; expressive language disorder, expressive–receptive language disorder, phonological disorder, and stuttering; autistic disorder; Asperger's disorder; attention-deficit hyperactivity disorder; disruptive behaviour disorders; (conduct disorder and oppositional defiant disorder); and separation anxiety disorder.

Further reading

Florian, L. and McLaughlin, M. J. (eds) (2008) *Disability Classification in Education*. Thousand Oaks, CA, Corwin Press.

This book looks critically at classifications of disability and disorder. Among the most stimulating chapters are, 'Perspectives and purposes of disability classification systems: implications for teachers and curriculum pedagogy' and 'International classification of functioning, disability and health for children and youth'.

World Health Organization (2007) *International Classification of Functioning, Disability and Health: Children and Youth Version*. Switzerland, Geneva, WHO.

As well as providing criteria for various categories of disability and disorder, this classification provides an insight into the thinking behind its development.

Chapter 7

Problems with assessment

This chapter examines assessments, especially intelligence tests, used in special education. It first considers the nature of intelligence and the characteristics of typical tests of intelligence. The chapter next looks at the assessment of intelligence with regard to reading disorder and to cognitive impairment. It then reviews criticisms of intelligence and its assessment that:

- the concept of intelligence and its testing are determinist;
- intelligence is associated with separate lower status schooling for some pupils;
- there are better alternatives.

The nature of intelligence and characteristics of tests

Intelligence has been said to concern various abilities. These are the ability to 'understand complex ideas', 'adapt effectively to the environment', 'learn from experience', 'engage in various forms of reasoning' and overcome obstacles by thinking about them (American Psychological Association Task Force, 1995). Individuals differ from one another in these abilities. If this conceptual outline is accepted, it follows that intelligent activity would involve related features such as seeing the essentials in a given situation and responding appropriately to them. There is debate about what responding appropriately might mean and what samples of such behaviour might be suitable to form part of any assessments of intelligence.

When intelligence tests are administered, there tend to be variations in the scores of the subtests that contribute to the overall score. Nevertheless, the scores on these subtests tend to correlate positively, so that a person who scores highly on one sub test tends to score highly on others. Interpretations of the structure of intelligence have been informed by statistical methods used in interpreting data. The technique of factor analysis and different methods of 'factoring' the correlations between sub-tests of intelligence have led to various interpretations of the structure of intelligence. This has included a theory that there is a general (g) factor representing what all the tests have in common. Others have emphasized the specific group factors such as memory or verbal comprehension.

Some critics maintain that the range of intelligence captured by intelligence tests is rather narrow and other types of intelligence have been mooted. For example, Howard Gardner (1983) suggested a multiple intelligence theory in his book, *Frames of Mind*. Initially he suggested the following intelligences:

- linguistic
- logical–mathematical
- musical
- bodily–kinaesthetic
- spatial
- interpersonal, and
- intrapersonal.

Gardner (1993) has subsequently developed the theory further and attempted to respond to criticisms including that the criteria for recognising the different intelligences are too subjective.

Richardson (1999) suggests that intelligence may be understood in the context of a series of nested 'regulations', that is, shaping influences. These are:

- genetic (caused by genes)
- genomic (determined by the DNA sequence)
- epigenetic (changes in gene expression occurring without change in DNA sequence)
- cognitive, and
- social.

(ibid. p. 177 for diagram summary)

Human social life takes over, transforms and extends existing regulations such as cognitive ones (ibid. p. 175). Intelligence is seen as quite dispersed and problems of interpretation emerge, it is suggested, when intelligence is believed to reside solely in one or a few levels (ibid. p. 189, paraphrased).

Among the different forms of intelligence test is *Raven's Progressive Matrices* (Raven *et al.*, 1998), which can be administered as a group test. A standard form comprises 60 designs in groups of 12. Each design has one piece omitted and several possible missing pieces are shown from which the correct one has to be chosen. As the test progresses, the logical judgement on which the correct response is based becomes more difficult. A coloured form is used for children aged 5 to 11 years or for people with cognitive impairment. Children whose physical or motor impairment may make some intelligence tests less accessible may be able to access *Raven's Progressive Matrices*, as the correct response can be made simply by pointing.

The 4th edition of the *Wechsler Intelligence Scale for Children* ® (*WISCIV*) *Integrated* (Kaplan *et al.*, 2004), is an individually administered intelligence test. There are ten core tests and five supplemental ones. These produce a full-scale intelligence quotient (IQ) and four 'indices' scores for verbal comprehension, perceptual reasoning, processing speed and working memory.

An intelligence test is standardized on a sample of individuals representative of the child being tested for example in terms of social background, gender and ethnicity. This enables scores achieved by the individual child to be compared with those of children of the same age. An important concept is that of IQ. Most modern intelligence tests have a deviation quotient and are standardized to produce distributions of IQs with a mean of 100 and a standard deviation of 15 points. Intelligence test scores can also be expressed in other ways including as percentile ranks. Although IQ scores do change over time in the same individual, generally, test scores are fairly stable during development (Moffit *et al.*, 1993).

Intelligence tests predict school performance quite well. They also predict scores on school achievement test moderately well, correlating about 0.5 with grade point average. School learning success is influenced by other factors, as well as intelligence including willingness to study (American Psychological Association, 1995, section 2).

Intelligence test scores are the best single predictor of the number of years an individual will spend in education. Correlations between test scores and the total number of years in education is about 0.55, suggesting differences in psychometric intelligence accounts for 30% of outcome variance. Among reasons for this is that high scoring individuals are likely to find education more rewarding.

Assessment of intelligence in special education

Assessments of intelligence are made in relation several types of disability and disorder. This section considers intelligence testing with regard to reading disorder and cognitive impairment.

Reading disorder

The *DSM-IV-TR* (American Psychiatric Association, 2000, pp. 51–53) defines reading disorder in terms of reading achievement being 'substantially below' what is expected, given the child's age, measured intelligence and education. Reading achievement is assessed according to reading accuracy, speed and comprehension, measured by individually administered standardized tests. To meet the criteria, reading disorder should 'significantly' hinder academic achievement or daily living activities requiring reading skills. Oral reading is characterized by 'distortions, substitutions or omissions' (ibid. p. 52) and both oral and silent reading tend to be slow and involve comprehension errors. Developmental delays in language may occur in association with reading disorder.

Reading achievement is usually taken to be 'substantially below' expectations when it is two or more standard deviations below the expected level. But one standard deviation may be considered sufficient, for example, where the disorder has had a significant impact on performance in the test of general intelligence (Fonagy *et al.*, 2002, p. 360).

The *DSM-IV-TR* (American Psychiatric Association, 2000, pp. 51–53) definition appears to support an IQ-achievement discrepancy view. Such a view defines reading impairment in terms of a discrepancy between a child's actual reading score and the reading score that would be predicted on the basis of chronological age or IQ (or both). Discrepancy scores are the difference between two test scores. The first is the score on a specified reading test. The second is the score predicted from the regression of reading performance on a measure of IQ (the correlation between reading and IQ). A specified sufficient discrepancy is taken to indicate underachievement in reading. Accordingly, a child could be considered to have reading disorder if he read as well or better than children of the same age but had a high IQ suggesting he should be doing better.

This view is increasingly challenged and there is growing consensus that reading disorder has to be associated with reading achievement being below age expectations. Beitchman and Young (1997), recommend that, if a child is not functioning below the expected level for age or grade, he is unlikely to require special help. He should not be considered to have a learning disorder, even though there may be a substantial IQ–achievement discrepancy.

Commercial assessments of 'dyslexia' standardized for the country concerned, often sample supposed component skills or necessary skills relating to reading. These include:

- rapid naming
- phonemic segmentation
- verbal fluency
- backwards digit span
- assessment of syllable, and
- phoneme deletions.

Cognitive impairment

Cognitive impairment in general

Cognitive impairment is referred to as 'mental retardation' (profound, moderate, severe and mild) in the United States of America, and as 'learning difficulty' (moderate, severe and profound) in England. It is identified with regard to two areas: intellectual functioning and adaptive behaviour/adaptive functioning (Algozzine and Ysseldyke, 2006b, p. 17). The *Diagnostic and Statistical Manual of Mental Disorders Fourth Edition Text Revision* (*DSM-IV-TR*) (American Psychiatric Association, 2000, e.g. p. 42) provides diagnostic criteria for mild, severe, moderate and profound 'mental retardation'. It stresses for all these that, although the criteria include IQ ranges, these are not the sole criterion. There must also be 'co-current deficits or impairments in present adaptive functioning . . . in at least two of the following areas: communication, self care, home living, social/interpersonal skills, use of community resources, self-direction, functional academic skills, work, leisure, health and safety.'

Commercial assessments of adaptive functioning (adaptive behaviour scales) set out a profile of strengths and weaknesses, such as those concerning personal and social skills. Profiles of adaptive behaviour may involve evaluations by parents, teachers and others. They relate to: daily living skills such as getting dressed; communication skills; and social skills, such as positive interactions with others (Algozzine and Ysseldyke, 2006b, p. 17). The American Association of Mental Deficiency suggested the skill areas can be considered in terms of: communication, community living, employment, functional academics, health and safety, home living, leisure, self-care and advocacy and social skills (ibid. pp. 21–23).

Expectations of the level and range of adaptive behaviours vary according to the child's age. Clearly, vocational and social responsibilities assume different contexts in later adolescence. For example, the *Vineland Adaptive Behaviour Scales (Vineland II)* (2nd edition) (Sparrow *et al.*, 2006) is intended to assess personal and social skills for every-day living from birth to adulthood. Information emerging from the scales covering communication, daily living skills, socialization and motor skills, also inform educational and treatment planning.

Mild cognitive impairment

In the United States of America, 'mild mental retardation' is associated with an IQ range of 50/55 to 70 (American Psychiatric Association, 2000, p. 42). There must be the co-occurring impairments in adaptive functioning mentioned earlier.

In England, 'moderate learning difficulties' is broadly equivalent in IQ terms to 'mild mental retardation'. The functional definition is also similar. Government guidance states that these pupils 'will have attainments significantly below expected levels in most areas of the curriculum, despite appropriate interventions. Their needs will *not* be able to be met by normal differentiation and the flexibilities of the National Curriculum' (Department for Education and Skills, 2003, p. 6, italics added). They 'have much greater difficulty than peers in acquiring basic literacy and numeracy skills and in understanding concepts. They may also have associated speech and language delay, low self-esteem, low levels of concentration and underdeveloped social skills' (ibid.).

Moderate to severe cognitive impairment

DSM-IV-TR (American Psychiatric Association, 2000, p. 42) relates 'moderate retardation' to IQ levels of 35/40 to 50/55. 'Severe retardation' is associated with IQ levels of 20/25 to 35/40. Consequently, the range for moderate to severe cognitive impairment is of IQ levels from 20/25 to 50/55. Most people with *moderate* mental retardation acquire communication skills in early childhood. With some supervision they, 'can attend to their personal care' (American Psychiatric Association, 2000, p. 43).

While benefiting from training in social and occupational skills, they are, 'unlikely to progress beyond second-grade level in academic subjects' (p. 43). Individuals with *severe* mental retardation tend to acquire little or no communicative speech in early childhood, but during the school age period may learn to talk and can learn 'elementary self care skills'. They profit to a limited degree from teaching in 'pre-academic subjects' such as 'simple counting' and can master skills such as sight-reading of some survival words (ibid. p. 43).

In England, 'severe learning difficulties' broadly correspond in IQ terms to the American 'moderate mental retardation' and 'severe mental retardation', that is an IQ range of 20/25–50/55 (Kushlick and Blunden, 1974). Government guidance (Department for Education and Skills, 2005, p. 6) (www.dfes.gov.uk/sen) indicates that, for much of their school careers, these pupils will be working below a level usually entered by a typically developing child at about the age of 5 to 6 years (ibid., paraphrased).

Lower IQ levels are associated with greater possibility of the child having a medical background condition. Around 40% of individuals with an IQ level of 70 have such a condition, but when individuals have an IQ below 50, then 80% have a medical background condition (Gillberg and Soderstrom, 2003).

Profound cognitive impairment

'Profound mental retardation' is defined (American Psychiatric Association, 2000, p. 42) according to limitations in both intellectual functioning and in adaptive behaviour. It is associated with an IQ range of below 20 or 25. Most children with profound mental retardation have an, 'identified neurological condition' accounting for the condition (p. 44). In early childhood, there are signs of impairments of sensory neural function.

Referring to possible childhood and adult development and provision, *DSM-IV-TR* states, 'Optimal development may occur in a highly structured environment with constant aid and supervision and an individualized relationship with a caregiver. Motor development and self-care and communication skills may improve if appropriate training is provided. Some can perform simple tasks in closely supervised and sheltered settings' (p. 44).

In England, a definition of 'profound and multiple learning difficulties' in government guidance states these pupils have 'severe and complex learning needs'. Additionally, '. . . they have other significant difficulties, such as physical disabilities or a sensory impairment. Pupils require a high level of support, both for their learning needs and for their personal care. They are likely to need sensory stimulation and a curriculum broken down into very small steps. Some pupils communicate by gesture, eye pointing or symbols, others by very simple language . . .' (Department for Education and Skills, 2003, p. 7).

Criticisms of assessments of intelligence

The deterministic nature of intelligence and intelligence testing

An aspect of the debate about intelligence and determinism is the relationships between intelligence and the respective contributions of heredity and the environment. Evidence is often cited from twin studies, such as the Minnesota Study of

Twins Reared Apart (Bouchard *et al.*, 1990). This involved bringing together from all over the world identical and non-identical twins brought up separately. They were given psychological and other tests, including tests of mental ability and personality.

Among the tests of mental ability were the *Wechsler Adult Intelligence Scales (WAIS)*. The total scores of the identical twins reared apart on the *WAIS* test battery correlated at 0.69. This very high correlation was not much lower than that of pairs of twins who have spent their lives together (0.88). In the *Raven's Progressive Matrices* the correlations of test scores (with a vocabulary scale added) for separately reared identical twins was 0.78, while for reared together identical twins it was 0.76.

Identical twins reared apart have: very similar intelligence to ones reared together, and very similar intelligence to each other. The effect of pairs of twins being placed in similar family environments was found to be small. Where some twins had lived together for some of their childhood, this was also found to have a very small effect. It was estimated from this study that genes contributed around 70% to the effect on intelligence differences and the environment contributed about 30%. In other words, when researchers look at the differences in mental abilities across a range of adult twins in Western developed countries, the difference between them in their mental abilities are affected by genes to the extent of 70%. Evidence from other research suggests that a very conservative estimate of genetic influence on intelligence differences would be about 50%.

Such studies have not been without critics. For example, in adopted twin experimental designs, it may be assumed that related individuals are being brought up in dissimilar environments, but this may not be known (Richardson, 1999, p. 71). Such criticisms may be speculative in that they may not re-examine the evidence, but simply raise the possibility of the contaminating effects of the environment of the findings of an existing study.

A book arguing against determinist interpretations of heredity in intelligence is *Not in Our Genes* (Rose *et al.*, 1984). The authors are critical of biological determinists, that is those who consider biology rather that the environment as being decisive in determining development. Biological determinists, the authors state, take the view that individuals' lives are 'strongly constrained by a relatively small number of internal causes, the genes for specific behaviours or for predisposition to these behaviours' (p. 289). The authors argue for 'dialectical explanations' (p. 11) rather than determinist ones.

The political intentions of the authors are set out clearly. Biological determinist ideas are seen as attempts to 'preserve the inequalities in our society' (Rose *et al.*, 1984, p. 15). Exposure of any fallacies in those ideas is part of a 'struggle to eliminate those inequalities and to transform our society' (ibid.). The authors point out the shortcomings of the data of Cyril Burt (pp. 101–106), an eminent British psychologist who contributed to intelligence theory and testing, and some of whose evidence was later discovered to be spurious (Hearnshaw, 1979).

A historical worry for some writers is the notion that intelligence testing is hand in glove with ideas of eugenics. Richardson (1999) links intelligence testing and German Nazis. The British and American founders of the intelligence testing movement were, 'mostly strong hereditarians and eugenists', seeing the IQ test a means of promoting their cause. They had been financially backed by the Pioneer Fund 'many of whose members have held explicitly racist, eugenicist and Pro-Nazi views' (p. 21). The assumptions underpinning views of intelligence are said to have influenced the testing of children in Britain at the age of 11 years and their subsequent education in 'modern', technical' or 'grammar' schools. Elsewhere, it is said, 'especially in Nazi Germany – essentially the same assumptions were affecting lives in a more fundamental way' (p. 35).

Richardson (1999) proposes that there is a 'genetic determinism at the core of IQ theory' forming a 'highly simplistic picture of human intelligence'. This has pervaded the minds of psychologists and those operating 'the institutions of education and employment' (p. 199). To ensure that the minds of these individuals are no longer pervaded in this way, Richardson calls for the banning of IQ testing (p. 201). This will 'lift the yoke of pessimism which IQ theory has placed on Western societies'. This might be a 'drastic step', but an 'internationally renowned psychologist' has also called for a moratorium on IQ testing until it is clearer what is being tested (ibid.).

Perhaps behind views about eugenics and sterilization lie worries about the more general role of heredity in relation to intelligence. There may be a concern that teachers and others could interpret the contribution of heredity as limiting. They might therefore make less effort to encourage the education and development of children including those with lower measured intelligence. However, the interaction between heredity and the environment is surely too complex to justify such a scenario.

Also, the straw man of biological determinism is hard to recognize in the work of modern school psychologists. There appears to be no substantiation for the notion that a modern-day psychologist or psychometrician regards heredity as forever fixing the potential of an individual without reference to influences of the environment. Indeed, a quite different response may be made. If genetic influences on intelligence differences are considerable, it can be argued it is particularly important to optimize environmental influences to aid development and learning.

Gould (1997) in *The Mismeasure of Man* takes a better-informed view. He admires the French psychologist Binet who developed the IQ test as 'a practical guide for identifying children whose poor performance indicated a need for special education – those who we would today call learning disabled or mildly retarded' (ibid. p. 182). Gould is supportive of 'antihereditarians' such as Binet for whom mental testing 'becomes a theory for enhancing potential through proper education' (p. 183). Binet's three principles of using IQ test meet with approval. These are that, firstly, the scores are a practical device and do not define anything exclusively innate or permanent. Secondly, the scale is a rough guide to 'identifying mildly retarded and learning disabled children who need special help', not a device 'for ranking normal children' (p. 185). Thirdly, emphasis is put on improvement through special training and low scores are not used to mark children as 'innately incapable' (ibid.).

Also, Gould (1997) disagrees that intelligence can be 'meaningfully abstracted as a single number capable of ranking all people on a linear scale of intrinsic and unalterable mental worth' (ibid. p. 20). He welcomes the discovery of 'genetic causes or influences' for conditions such as obsessive-compulsive disorder (p. 33) and has 'an agnostic attitude' towards mental testing in general (p. 40). He celebrates the value of identifying 'inborn biological bases' for conditions such as autism that were once considered psychogenetic (ibid. p. 32).

Intelligence testing and separate schooling

It is not difficult to see why intelligence testing is criticized by those supporting educational mainstreaming. It has been claimed that assumptions about the effectiveness of separate special schools, 'largely built on notions of the importance of nature over nurture', rested on a view of 'inherited and immutable intelligence' (Thomas and Loxley, 2007, pp. 36–37). It is maintained there is a historical affinity between perceived student educability and separate schooling. In this view, students' educability seen as 'fundamentally circumscribed by a global, determinate intellectual capacity' is related to 'policy regimes which construct a differentiated system of schooling, in which some students are denied access to high-status forms of provision' (Skidmore, 2004, p. 114).

However, the idea that educability is circumscribed by intellectual 'capacity' is difficult to maintain, based on the heritabilty evidence of intelligence tests. Also, policy regimes with differentiated schools are not necessarily typified by 'denying' provision, whether it is high status or not. For example, in the United States of America and elsewhere, there are differentiated schools of many kinds, but they are not necessarily seen as a denial of choice, often the opposite.

Pupils can attend separate schools according to religious belief, or sex, as well as disability and disorder. The assumption that a separate school is a lower status school is unexplained. For example, parents and pupils may see a special school with small classes, expert staff, rich resources, specialist curricula, supportive organization, distinctive pedagogy and expensive facilities as high status (Farrell, 2006a).

Limitations of assessments of cognitive impairment and alternatives

Judgements of the progress of a special child are made with care. If special educators compare the progress of special children with those of typically developing children, they could be thought to be emphasizing deficits. If they compare, say, the motor and coordination progress of a pupil with developmental coordination disorder with other pupils with the same disorder, special educators might be considered to be lowering expectations of progress. In practice, judgements are made in both ways. (Please also see Farrell, 2009b, the entry on 'progress'.)

The identification of pupils with mild cognitive impairment is open to criticism because schools and others cannot always agree a definition. Criteria might include levels of attainment in English and mathematics and other curriculum areas that would be expected. They might include cognitive levels as indicated by standardized tests, or measures of difficulty in understanding concepts. An interesting idea is that 'dynamic assessment' might additionally be used where, as the term suggests, assessment is

made during activities. This seeks to measure the responsiveness of an individual to teaching and practice (Bransford *et al.*, 1986). As well as offering a baseline assessment, it provides information on the degree and form of assistance the child needs in order to reach a higher level of performance, and how he responds to such help.

It has been argued (Greenspan, 2006) that there are limitations with an IQ-based definition of mild cognitive impairment, for example, because it does not provide a broad enough picture of what might be considered intelligence. There are also limitations with functional-based definitions because they confound mental retardation with other forms of disability. A suggested alternative is to ground a definition in its 'natural taxon' (a taxonomic group such as a class/classification). This taxon would be determined from the behaviours of people widely considered to have mental retardation, key aspects being various forms of vulnerability.

More broadly, in 2002, the American Association on Intellectual and Developmental Disabilities (AAIDD) agreed a supports-based definition. This presents mental retardation as a condition that can be enhanced by the provision of supports rather than as a more static disability. However, it is difficult to envisage the required support being allocated fairly unless it is based on some judgement of what is required that ultimately refers to characteristics of the person deemed to require the support. Nevertheless, the notion of support provision could inform and clarify existing definitions of cognitive impairment and might also suggest suitable types of pedagogy.

Conclusion

Intelligence tests constitute part of the assessment of types of disability and disorder including cognitive impairment and reading disorder. It is sometimes claimed that intelligence is about fundamentally circumscribed capacity that can constrain aspirations about a child's ability to learn. However, this view does not take account of evidence that there are substantial environmental contributions to intelligence differences and that heredity and environment interact.

Views about intelligence neither support nor contradict arguments concerning separate schooling. This is a question of where the child will learn and develop better. Functional, support-based and other assessments that are considered along with assessments of intelligence give a fuller picture of a child's strengths and weaknesses.

Summary statement: assessment

Functional, support based and other assessments including assessments of intelligence contribute productively to a fuller picture of a child's abilities and skills.

Thinking points

Readers may wish to consider:

*   the strengths and weakness of arguments concerning the use of assessments in general and intelligence tests, in particular;
*   the relationships between assessments and the use of criteria for classifications of disabilities and disorders.

Key text

Gould, S. J. (1997, 2nd edition) *The Mismeasure of Man.* Harmondsworth, Penguin.
This well-written book is critical of the idea of exclusively inherited, unchangeable general intelligence.

Further reading

American Psychological Association (1994) *Intelligence: Knowns and Unknowns.* Washington, APA (www.lrainc.com/swtaboo/taboos/apa_01.html).
Compiled by a task force of the American Psychological Association, this report provides a clear picture of what psychologists currently agree is known about intelligence, and what is not known.
Kaplan, R. M. and Saccuzzo, D. P. (2005) *Psychological Testing: Principles, Applications and Issues.* Belmont, CA, Thompson Wadworth.
Sternberg, R. R. J. (ed.) (2008) *Handbook of Intelligence.* Cambridge, Cambridge University Press.
This text provides comprehensive and up to date coverage of many aspects of intelligence.
Mitchell, D. (ed.) (2004c) *Special Educational Needs and Inclusive Education: Major Themes in Education, Volume 3: Assessment and Teaching Strategies.* London and New York, Routledge Falmer.
A selection of already published articles from journals, some of which concern assessment strategies.

Chapter 8

Negative effects of labelling

This chapter considers whether labelling associated with special education has negative consequences for children. It examines interpretative sociological perspectives, labelling theory and identity. The chapter presents the case that labelling, including unnecessary medical labelling, can be negative. It considers terms historically associated with cognitive impairment and how they have changed. The chapter examines both the negative and positive labelling of children, parents and staff connected with special schools. Finally, the positive labelling of disabilities and disorders is considered.

Interpretative sociological perspectives, labelling theory and identity

Dawe (1970) describes two types of sociologies. The first concerns social systems. It specifies social constraint as necessary for the well-being of society and of the individual and regards the social system as being 'ontologically prior' to its participants. The second type of sociology is interpretative. It sees individuals as autonomous and able to create a 'truly human' social order only when liberated from outside constraints. In this view, society is regarded as a creation of its members, a product of their 'construction of meaning' and of the 'action and relationships' by which they try to impose this meaning on their situation.

One of the perspectives within the interpretative position is interactionism. In interactionist perspectives, subjective reality is important. Consequently, the way a participant sees his own actions and situation is a key area of investigation and analysis. The process by which individuals 'construct' their actions is an important focus for the interactionist sociologist. Language is central in enabling individuals to reflect on their physical and social world.

Labelling theory, a collection of ideas related to an interactionist sociological perspective, has been developed mainly in the area of criminology (e.g. Farrell, 1990). Deviant behaviour is seen as having 'the characteristics of a transaction between the deviant person and another or others' (Walker, 2007, p. 368). Deviance then is not seen as a quality of a person's behaviour, but as an interaction between the person manifesting the behaviour and the response of others (Becker, 1963, p. 9, paraphrased). This does not necessarily lead to the diminishing of the harm that criminal behaviour might incur. It focuses on the creation of the deviant identity over and above the actions that might lead to such an identity being ascribed.

Personal identity, an important aspect of self-valuing and self-esteem, is affected by the perceptions of oneself and of others. Identity has been an important element of the social model in shifting focus of the apparent location of difficulties from the individual to such factors as social arrangements and the attitudes of others.

An aspect of labelling relates to personal identity. Where individuals with a disability or disorder identify themselves with others with disabilities and disorders, this can lead to positive affirmations of the self and a positive sense of identity. In this context, the term 'disability culture' may be used. Arguing for a positive identity for impairment can be seen as asserting the 'value and validity' of the life of a person with an impairment (Swain and French, 2000, p. 578). It is suggested, 'In affirming the positive identity of being impaired, disabled people are actively repudiating the dominant value of normality' (ibid.).

Regarding young disabled people in modern society, it has been said, 'The growth of disability pride suggests that disabled people do not want to be other than they are. They are not rejecting disability as an identity or trying to escape the biological realities of impairment' (Hughes *et al.*, 2005, p. 7).

It has been suggested, however (Shakespeare, 2006, p. 70), that such views might limit the range of sources that an individual might draw on in affirming their identity. It seems to imply that impairment inevitably defines personal identity and that disability identity is an unquestioned inevitability. Instead, it can be argued that disability politics offers a new opportunity to inform identity but not an inevitable one (ibid., paraphrased).

The negative labelling of special children

Negative labelling in general

As mentioned, labelling theory developed in the area of criminology. It can therefore be relevant where types of disabilities and disorders sometimes overlap with criminal behaviour, as with severe conduct disorder. But labelling has also been considered in relation to other disabilities and disorders. The whole area of disability and disorder may be considered by some to be a form of negative labelling. It has been claimed, '. . . American professionals are orientated towards distinction-making; they compulsively stress the importance of normality and are crazy about labelling' (Brantlinger, 2006, p. 234). Furthermore, it is suggested, 'that children are unhappy with labels and about being stuck in special education has been well documented' (ibid.).

Attempts have been made to interpret the role of terminology of public perception and attitudes to people with 'learning difficulties' (Eayrs *et al.*, 1993). In the area of 'learning difficulties', there is sometimes resistance to medical or psychological labelling associated with assessment or diagnosis (Gillman *et al.*, 2000). One aspect of labelling has been associated with unequal relationships. It is related to powerful groups being able to define the ways less powerful groups are perceived and relatedly how they are treated (Eayrs *et al.*, 1993).

It is said that negative labelling associated within special education damages children's self-esteem, and lowers the aspirations of teachers, parents and others. If a child or young person is seen solely in terms of a category such as 'mild cognitive impairment' and nothing else, there is a worry that the term might constrain opportunities.

Indeed, in the 1920s, Byelorussian psychologist Lev Vygotsky (1896–1934) saw the importance of recognizing strengths as well as weaknesses. He states that a child who is blind should be educated, not as a blind child, but first and foremost as a child. Otherwise, there is a risk that special pedagogy is completely focused on the disability or disorder alone (Vygotsky, [1924]/1993, p. 83). He argues for recognizing a child's strengths, not only his weakness (Vygotsky, [1925–6]/1993, p. 68 and [1927]/1993, p. 56). He sought to construct the educational process on the basis of compensatory drives. This involves ensuring the child's strengths and concentrated on compensating for the 'defect', and selecting in proper sequence tasks that eventually shape the whole personality 'from a new standpoint' (p. 57).

Bromfield *et al.* (1986) found labelling to have a negative effect when looking at children's judgements and attributions with regard to the label 'mentally retarded'. They argue that constraining labelling leads to teachers having lower aspirations for pupils that, in turn, lead to underachievement.

Shakespeare (2006, p. 71) refers to the phenomena of 'identity spread'. Through this, it is suggested that personality (and other aspects of identity such as ethnicity and gender) can be subsumed under a label of impairment that comes to dominate interactions with others. It is important that teachers and others recognize the label is not the whole child. The things the child is good at, as well as those he finds difficult, need to be borne in mind.

This mixture of weaknesses and strengths is used to ensure progress, and personal development is encouraged as well as possible. Expectations are stretched in good schools by the development of challenging aspirations for achievement based on a wide range of information. This includes information on how well other children are doing in comparison, how well the child progressed previously, the expectation of schools where best practice is found and other data.

Medical labelling

Some labels seem to create and perpetuate an excessively medical view of underperformance. The Greek term 'dyslexia' suggests something rather more than a severe difficulty with reading. Pupils considered to have dyslexia may be 'diagnosed' rather than assessed, be 'treated' rather than receive suitable provision, and attend a 'clinic' instead of a place where they get help learning to read. Such terminology may create an impression of illness for what is essentially a severe literacy problem.

Perhaps the expression used in the United States of America is more apt, 'reading disorder'. Even the 'disorder' part of this expression may be argued to be somewhat medical. But it can also be maintained that it indicates a difficulty with reading that is far in excess of run-of-the-mill difficulties. Other disorders are sometimes given Greek medical sounding appellations, for example, 'dyspraxia' for development coordination disorder and 'dyscalculia' for mathematics disorder. These considerations influence those who argue that labels relating to disability be abandoned altogether and concentrate more on the person as a whole and on his social experiences, taking a view that disability is socially created (e.g. Oliver, 1992, pp. 20–22).

Earlier terminology

The language of special education

Different 'discourses' have been suggested in relation to disability and disorder, such as medical, lay, charity, rights and corporate ones (Fulcher, 1989, p. 26). In *Bad-Mouthing*, Corbett (1996), examines what she considers to be the dominant discourse of 'special needs' relating this to the voice of 'enlightened modernity' and professional patronage. She suggests this discourse 'needs to be challenged by competing voices' (p. 7). These include the different strands of 'disability culture' including theorizing, poetry, drama and personal narrative, and the language of rights (p. 95). 'Special needs' is seen as socially constructed and language is considered to have been developed 'to sustain, contain and control it' (p. 7).

Corbett (1996) maintains people's use of language shapes perception and can be changed. She states that, by recognizing the pros and cons of past special language, 'we are placed in a better position to select whatever was useful and discard a vocabulary which holds us back' (ibid. p. 8). Corbett takes the view that, 'Language is a source of power and control and, as such, to be contested: words need to be won' (ibid. p. 46). It is suggested there ought to be a 'deconstruction of existing hierarchies' leading to a 'more liberating and open level of debate' (ibid. p. 42).

Such a view, that groups of people can corral language and make it do what they want, is difficult to sustain. It is not supported by a consideration of the way disabilities and disorders have been spoken about in the past and the perceived need to change terminology. A brief consideration of the British context may illustrate.

Terminology and cognitive impairment

The terminology used in the past to refer to individuals that are now considered to have a disability or disorder is instructive in many ways. The British context of the shifting terminology for what is presently known as 'learning difficulties' (cognitive impairment) demonstrates such changes. In 1913, the British government passed an Act, the Mental Deficiency Act, which applied to England. It defined 'mental deficiency' as '. . . a condition of arrested or incomplete development of mind . . .'. Mental deficiency was subdivided into four classifications: idiots, imbeciles, morons and moral defectives. Leaving aside 'moral defectives', the three definitions were as follows.

Idiots were, 'persons in whose case there exists mental defectiveness to such a degree that they are incapable of guarding themselves against common physical dangers'. Such children in the early twenty-first century were referred to as having 'profound cognitive impairment' or in England as having 'profound learning difficulties'. Under the Act, an 'imbecile' was a person, '. . . in whose case mental defectiveness, though not amounting to idiocy, is yet so pronounced that they are incapable of managing themselves and their affairs or, in the case of children, of being taught to do so'. Today, these children are referred to as having 'moderate to severe cognitive impairment' or in England 'severe learning difficulties'. A 'moron' was mildly mentally defective and would today be considered as having, 'mild cognitive impairment' or in England, 'moderate learning difficulties'.

The 1913 Mental Deficiency Act and subsequent amendments were replaced by the Mental Health Act 1959, which applied to England or Wales. This used the concepts of 'mental disorder' and divided it into four categories: mental illness, psychopathic disorder, severe subnormality and subnormality. In the sphere of education, regulations in 1959 following the Education Act of 1944 listed various handicapping categories. These included 'educationally sub-normal'. Children who were 'severely sub-normal' were considered to be unable to benefit from education in schools, but were deemed the responsibility of health services and were educated in training centres, special care units and elsewhere.

The Education (Handicapped Children) Act 1970 moved responsibility for these children from the health authorities to local education authorities. The children were then considered, 'educationally sub-normal – severe' to distinguish them from other children in the educationally subnormal category who became 'educationally sub-normal – moderate'.

The Warnock Report of 1978 adopted the expression 'special educational needs'. Subsequent Acts including the Education Act 1996 followed the same terminology. Within this broad heading, categories of cognitive impairment are 'profound learning difficulties' (profound cognitive impairment), severe learning difficulties (severe to moderate cognitive impairment), and moderate earning difficulties (mild cognitive impairment) (Department of Education and Skills, 2005).

The implications of even such a brief historical review are revealing. If one tries to walk back into the past, when terms such as 'idiot' and 'imbecile' were initially used, there is no suggestion that the terms were derogatory or had negative connotations. They appear to have been attempts to use terms to convey an individual's different typical capabilities of keeping himself safe. The fact that these terms are in the present day almost exclusively terms of abuse appears to have come about by the associations of those words with conditions or states of development ('mental defectiveness') which society feared. New terms were introduced such as 'educationally sub-normal', but these too soon acquired a negative association. Later, expressions such as 'profound mental retardation' entered terminology. These too have become negative as the use of 'retard' as a term of abuse in the United States of America indicates. The expression, 'cognitive impairment' is presently becoming more widely used in some countries such as Australia.

In India it is said the 'influence' of the World Health Organization and the United Nations led to changes in terminology used to define disabling conditions. Out went, 'retarded', 'crippled' and 'lame'. In came 'mentally challenged', 'visually impaired' and 'physically impaired'. But, 'In spite of this change in language, the social and cultural perception of society did not undergo change' (Ghia, 2002, p. 92).

All this suggests that it is the attitudes of society to individuals with cognitive impairments that is the constant, and that changing the language does not change the attitudes. This runs counter to the view that a key mark of progress is to manage the terms society uses so that what people think becomes modified too. Changing the language to change the way people think appears not to have had much effect. It appears not to be negative labelling that is influential, but negative perceptions that influence the connotations and use of language (Farrell, 1998, pp. 16–17).

The interaction between perception and language is of course far from straightforward. It may be that negative perceptions colour the terms that are used so that the terms themselves acquire some of the negativity. Changing terms periodically might be partly explainable from this standpoint.

Children, parents and staff involved with special schools: negative and positive labelling

A United Kingdom charity pressing for mainstreaming lists reasons against 'segregated' schooling. These included that:

> The discrimination inherent in segregated schooling *offends the human dignity* of the child and is capable of undermining or even *destroying the capacity of the child to benefit from educational opportunities*.
>
> Segregated schooling appeases the human tendency to *negatively label* and isolate those perceived as different . . .
>
> Segregated schooling perpetuates *discrimination, devaluation, stigmatisation, stereotyping, prejudice, and isolation* – the very conditions which disabled adults identify as among the biggest barriers to respect, participation and a full life. (Centre for Studies in Inclusive Education, 2003, italics added)

In this example, it appears that special schools 'offend' a child's 'human dignity'; destroy a child's 'capacity to benefit from educational opportunities'; are involved in 'devaluing and distancing'; and perpetuate 'discrimination, devaluation, stigmatization, stereotyping, prejudice, and isolation'. The point that special schools might appease a tendency to 'negatively label' children in the context of this tirade against special schools has a wonderful unrecognized irony.

The negative labelling of special schools may reflect elements of ideology outlined by Minogue (1995, p. 17). The past history of provision for special children may be presented as the oppression of these pupils. Instead of seeking to tackle any particular examples of dissatisfaction with special schools in the real world, specific discontents might be gathered into a vision of structurally determined 'oppression'. Supporters might seek to mobilize adults with disabilities into a struggle against the perceived oppressive system. Liberation, it is expected, would be achieved when all pupils attend mainstream schools.

This is not to say that there are not adults who looking back on their education in special schools do so with unhappiness. There are undoubtedly adults with disabilities or disorders who were educated in mainstream schools who look back in a similar way. But the response for some is not to examine particular special schools or particular experiences in them and seek to change what was not good. It is to assume all special schools must be a bad thing and to close one's ears to anyone who has had a different experience or who holds a different view.

Among confused and conflicting messages concerning special education from the New Labour government in the United Kingdom, a negative view of the schools can be discerned. Warnock (2006, p. viii) points out:

> For years government ministers and civil servants have paid grudging lip-service to special schools: 'We recognize that there will always be a place for some special schools, for children with the most profound and complex disabilities . . .'. This has put the special schools firmly at the bottom of the pile, not something that any sane parent would choose for her child; and it has perpetuated the unexamined assumption that all parents and all children prefer mainstream education. (p. viii)

The negative labelling of special schools implies not just a poor view of the schools. It also demeans the children educated there, their parents for choosing the special school, the staff who work there and managers and governors who run the school. While purporting to respect special children and their parents, it ignores their voice. Or, at the very least, it takes the voice of some who do not want special schools to be the only voices worth listening to. It then elides these voices into an abstract statement of supposed 'rights' in the manner described by Minogue (1995).

Yet pupils in special schools have very different accounts of their experiences. Taking the example of England, this is indicated in comments reported by a government working group (Department for Education and Skills, 2003, pp. 152–170). To take just a few examples, pupils who had moved from mainstream to special schools made comments such as the following about their special school experience:

- 'friendlier'
- 'nicer, my mum's really pleased I am here now'
- 'doesn't get so wound up about the way I behave'
- 'I get my therapy now – I never got it at Y school'
- 'more friends – I can walk to school with them'.

Elsewhere, the voice of pupils from special schools has been reported (Farrell, 2006, pp. 41–43). These include the results of a survey carried out and analysed by pupils in a special school, demonstrating that 55 of 62 pupils would not want to return to mainstream schools. In another school, pupils speak very positively of the provision. One boy states, 'I think it's a very good school. I think it should be all over the country and all over the world for pupils with behaviour difficulty problems ...' (ibid. p. 41). Others writing as adults give powerful accounts of the transformation their special school made to their lives (ibid. pp. 42–43).

Parents too speak with great appreciation of special school education. Some contributed to a special schools working group (Department for Education and Skills, 2003, pp. 123–151). Among the advantages of special schools, parents stated were positive expectations; no difficulties administering medicines; a fully accessible physical environment; better behaviour management; and access to external specialists. In a survey of parents (Wilmot, 2006), issued to all parents with a child educated in a shire county special school for children with 'moderate learning difficulties' (mild cognitive impairment), 93% felt that the special school was the best available option and 96% said they would prefer the pattern of special school provision to stay as it was, rather than have more mainstreaming.

From other sources (Farrell, 2006, pp. 27–28; 31–37) parents speak and write deeply felt endorsements of the education and provision their child receives in special school. Parents from one special school spoke of their great satisfaction with the school. One stated: 'My son was in a mainstream unit for two and a half years. He is autistic. It was a disaster.' By contrast, in the special school 'It was completely different. They look past the disabilities' (Farrell, 2006, p. 33). Parents' contribution to annual reviews of statements, responses to parent questionnaires, recorded interviews with parents, letters, newsletters and personal communications support this picture (ibid. pp. 33–37).

Positive labelling of disabilities and disorders

Labelling is a complex and paradoxical process (Shakespeare and Erickson, 2000) and single dimensional accounts emphasizing only negative aspects and stigma do not capture this complexity. MacMillan *et al.* (1974) reviewed research literature concerning five areas of possible negative labelling in relation to children then considered 'mentally retarded'. These were the child's self-concept, and his future vocational adjustment, rejection by peers, attitudes of his family, and the expectations of teachers. They found little support for the view that children were stigmatized by being labelled, 'retarded' (ibid.).

Kurtz *et al.* (1977) conducted a study comparing labelled and non-labelled pre school children. The label was found to produce a positive effect in terms of teachers showing less social distance. Gottlieb (1986) maintained that the observable behaviour of children could lead to them being negatively regarded by peers, irrespective of whether a child was labelled as 'retarded' by the school. If inappropriate behaviour is more noticeable in an ordinary school, it was argued, then attempts to include pupils with mental retardation would be likely to lead to them being ostracized by peers than would education in separate provision (ibid.).

Even when labelling is shown to have a positive effect, the interpretation of research can still show reluctance to accept the findings or the consequences. Vlachou (1997, p. 41), after reviewing some of the research demonstrating the majority shows positive effects of labelling, concludes, 'The notion of positive effects . . . is quite disturbing'. She asks, 'How 'positive' can interactions be that include notions of pity, over protectiveness, dependency, 'special dispensation' and the perpetuation of 'sick roles'?'

Finding that labelling has a positive effect can certainly be 'disturbing' to anyone convinced it can only be negative. For Vlachou (1997, citing eight references), the definitive answer to her questions comes from 'numerous' disabled people. Furthermore, she is convinced the studies were misguided in that they, 'isolated the creation and formation of labelling from the institutional practices of the society that created such labels in the first place' and paid no attention to the 'reasons and the social roots behind the creation of such labels' (ibid. p. 41).

Contrary to such speculations, pupils attending special schools often speak very positively as a government report in England shows. One says, 'When I moved to the special school, I found I could really do my work. Everything was presented in a way I understood' (Department for Education and Skills, 2003, p. 160). Pupils who had moved from mainstream school to special school had many positive comments about the special schools. They say these schools were 'friendlier'. They state that the school 'Doesn't get wound up about the way I behave' or 'Doesn't make a fuss about my medication'. Pupils report they have 'More friends – I can walk to school with them'. Another states, 'I get my therapy now, I never got it at Y school' (ibid. p. 157). Following many such comments, the report concludes, 'Although some literature on pupils' perceptions of education suggests that they may feel special schools to be stigmatizing, no negative messages emerged from our focus groups' (ibid. p. 169).

Other sources paint a similar picture. Far from feeling that 'emotional disabilities' was a negative label, a pupil says of his special school, New Rush Hall near London (www.nrhs.redbridge.sch.uk), 'When I'm here with a bunch of boys that's got emotional disabilities, I feel more comfortable and more confident'. On leaving school, this student successfully applied to, and was accepted on, a course at a local college (source, New Rush Hall DVD 'Partnership in Practice'). (For further examples, see Farrell, 2006a, pp. 38–45.)

Neither do parents associate special education and special schooling with negative labelling of their children. Some parents feel strongly that special schools offer 'a much less restrictive environment for pupils with intimate and health care needs' (Department for Education and Skills, 2003, p. 142). Parents in a focus group reported, 'their lives and those of their children had been saved by residential special school placements' (ibid. p. 138). Among advantages to special schools, parents noted positive expectations, no difficulties administering medicines, a fully accessible physical environment, better behaviour management and better access to specialists (ibid. p. 134).

For some parents of children with autism, a diagnosis and a label can feel disempowering and lead them to worry about the future, while for others it can lead to better understanding of the condition (Hodge, 2005). Some parents find the recognition of their child's disability difficult to deal with, while for other a label is a helpful signpost to other parents and support groups. A parent states, 'Our son went to Brooklands School with no language/no diagnosis/severe learning difficulties and very little understanding of the world he lived in and within one year of being within this amazing school with its fantastic staff he is now a delightful, happy, confident, bright child with a diagnosis of autistic spectrum disorder' (letter from parents to author, 2005, personal communication). (For other examples of parents' views, please see Farrell, 2006a, pp. 27–37.)

Conclusion

It is sometimes suggested that labelling associated with special education has negative impacts on children. These are said to include the unnecessary medicalizing of educational difficulties. However, it may not be always language that negatively effects perception, but perception may negatively affect language, making it important to pay attention to perceptions and experiences as well as being sensitive to language. Parents may welcome labelling that enables them to share common experiences with other families and gain access to support and other resources. The negative labelling of special schools and the children and parents associated with them can be countered by examples of positive labelling.

Summary statement: labelling

Special educators strive to ensure the positive labelling of children receiving special education, their parents and others working in special education.

Thinking points

Readers may wish to consider:

* the ways in which labels are developed and how they acquire their connotations;
* how ideas on labelling might apply to children, parents and schools.

Key text

Meighan, R. and Harber, C. (2007) *A Sociology of Educating.* London, Continuum.
   Chapter 25 provides an introduction to labelling theory and relates this to life chances.

Further reading

Corbett, J. (1996) *Bad Mouthing: The Language of Special Needs.* London, Routledge.
   This book concerns the language of 'special needs'. It suggests the discourse of special needs could be expanded by including elements from disability arts and elsewhere.

Chapter 9

Professional limitations

While many admire the work of educators and other professionals connected with special education, criticism is not unknown. This chapter examines allegations that often-unrecognized forces may be at work in special education running counter to the well-being of special children. These forces include professional self-interest and isolationism. The possible overuse of medication is another concern, perhaps related to tendency, not always justified, to see children's difficulties in a medical light. These are considered and possible responses discussed.

Professional self-interest

Professional self-interest is sometimes presented as part of a range of factors that support special education because of benefits to themselves. In considering who benefits from high stakes testing and hierarchies, Brantlinger (2006, pp. 209–219) intimates that there are benefits to test producers, transglobal capitalists, media moguls, politicians and political pundits and conservatives. Among conservatives are advocates of school privatization, enterprising school superintendents, members of the professional middle classes, and professionals and the professions.

It is suggested that, the swelling of an underclass 'at risk' or 'with needs' means employment security and extended job opportunities for credentialed professionals who have the expertise needed in the expanding social service bureaucracies' (Brantlinger, 2006, p. 218).

Over-identification of disorders and disabilities

Some criticisms of professionals working with special children point out a possible conflict of interest. This lies in the fact that professionals are involved both in identifying special children and providing services for them. Furthermore, some disabilities and disorders are more difficult to identify and assess than others. At worst, these two issues and other factors, it is suggested, might lead to professionals over-identifying special children. Other factors might also encourage over-identification or unjustifiable identification.

An example is reading disorder. Widely used criteria for reading disorder specify that reading achievement is 'substantially below' what is expected given the child's age, measured intelligence and education (American Psychiatric Association, 2000, pp. 51–53). However, there is not always agreement about what 'substantially below' means in terms of assessments used. (Please also see the entry on 'Reading disorder' in Farrell, 2009b.)

The rapid increase in the apparent incidence of attention deficit hyperactivity disorder (ADHD) is a further concern. There have been suggestions that this might relate to social pressures on parents to accept such a label, rather than the implication that they are ineffective parents (Lloyd *et al.*, 2006). The increasing use of medication for ADHD (see later section) has raised worries that the marketing of medication by drug companies may be inflating demand. Other disorders have also apparently increased.

A continuum of 'autistic spectrum disorder' is proposed on which exists autistic-like features of different degrees of severity. The breadth of this notion of a continuum may have contributed to increases in identification and to the apparent increases in the incidence of the disorder.

The fact that professionals identify, and provide for, various conditions and that some conditions are difficult to identify, can raise doubts that professionals are being as critical as they might be. It may be suspected that some professionals may be identifying conditions because they do not give enough credence to the context. Psychologists may be thought to be too quick to identify a child's 'behavioural difficulty' without considering sufficiently the classroom context that might be contributing to the apparent problem. In others words, the psychologist might be assuming too early a within-child explanation before exploring sufficiently systems explanations. Some critics worry that professionals may be resistant to criticisms because they have such a vested interest in maintaining their client base. It has been suggested, that, '. . . professionals and practitioners have vested interests in the expansion and development of special education' (Tomlinson, 1982, p. 5).

The dichotomy that is sometimes presented of a social view of disability and a 'medical model' is well known. It may reflect a mistrust of professionals taking a very predominantly individual view of disability and disorder. On the other hand, parents and pupils may speak well of the work of professionals (Farrell, 2006a).

The possible over-identification of children as having disabilities and disorders does not relate just to concerns about professional self-interest. But steps can be taken to avoid over-identification and these may contribute to greater trust among professionals, parents, schools and others.

Perhaps the most important constructive step is seeking common agreement on the nature of different types of disabilities and disorders. In this respect, the approach taken in England is muddled. Schools use a progress–resources-related approach to identifying 'special educational needs'. Broad categories are used, depending on the resource level. Children with special educational needs who progress well enough with support provided within the school are said to be at the 'school action' level. Where support and advice from outside are required (such as the involvement of a school psychologist), the child is said to be at the 'school action plus' stage. If progress is still not maintained, a 'statement' of special educational needs may be provided, specifying the provision required (Department of Education and Skills, 2001).

There are several problems. Firstly, and notoriously, 'need' including 'special educational need' is very difficult to pin down. The child 'needs' support for a reason. This relates to the child having 'learning difficulty', which calls for special educational provision to be made. The use of the term 'need' fudges the reason why the need exists, that is, because the child has a learning difficulty. At the same time, schools are expected to be able to specify the children they are educating in terms of various categorical classifications such as 'moderate learning difficulties' (mild cognitive impairment) and 'specific learning difficulties – dyslexia' (reading disorder) (Department of Education and Skills, 2005).

In the United States of America, the disability codes are clearer. These specify the various types of disorder and disability. If a child has one or more of these disorders, and they get in the way of his education, he may be entitled to special education.

Whatever the legal definitions, it needs to be clear what is being referred to when types of disability and disorder are concerned. Where criteria are used, these can help develop agreement. The *Diagnostic and Statistical Manual of Mental Disorders Fourth Edition Text Revision* (American Psychiatric Association, 2000) provides criteria for several disorders. This does not resolve difficulties of interpretation and practice, but it is a step towards creating agreement on what is meant when referring, for example, to 'autism' or 'developmental coordination disorder'.

Where guidance on this is provided, local discussion is likely to help ensure that interpretations of the criteria and guidance are robust. This might involve discussion among parents, professionals, school administrators and others. Over-identification may also be reduced if funding bodies avoid unquestioned links between the identification of increasing numbers of special pupils and increased school funding.

Historical interpretations

Historical examples draw on different information and come to different interpretations of professional motivation. On the negative side, there have been criticisms suggestive of professional self-interest. Thomas Braidwood an early worker in deaf education from the 1790s used lip reading and writing to teach deaf children to speak and read. But he has been criticized for his 'secretiveness' (Pritchard, 1963, p. 15). An American visitor in 1815 found teachers in deaf institutions in Edinburgh, London and Birmingham had all been sworn to secrecy about their methods.

Indeed, Laurent Clerc (1785–1869), who lost his hearing in infancy, regarded the secretiveness of pioneers of deaf education as a refusal to share their methods to benefit the deaf community (cited in Lane, 1984). Tomlinson (1982), taking a sociological perspective, examining social control is suspicious of humanitarian and Christian reformist interpretations of developments. She presents evidence and arguments that professional rivalries and vested interests were operating. Social control was seen as a predominant feature of apparently benevolent provision.

On the positive side, James Kerr, medical officer to the Bradford School Board from 1893, where he selected children for the first special classes for the 'mentally handicapped', has been praised for his 'wealth of compassion' (Pritchard, 1963, p. 129). Seguin (1812–1880) believed that the work of the pioneers of deaf education contributed to the integration of deaf people into a hearing society (Safford and Safford, 1996, p. 32). Thomas Barnardo, founder of homes for destitute boys in England, looked after children in his own home (Cole, 1989, p. 9).

It has been said that pioneers of education outside the mainstream were 'motivated by a desire for a more orderly society and a genuine concern for the socially, physically and mentally disadvantaged' (Hurt, 1988, p. 189). Cole (1989) pointedly challenges 'some aspects of recent sociological interpretations of special education's history' (p. 7). Accepting that there is some substance to the social control hypothesis in the history of special education, he argues that humanitarian motives predominated. He maintains, 'The moral belief and liberal humanitarianism of many contemporaries should not be underestimated in the late Victorian age, or for that matter in any period afterwards' (ibid.).

Complications of determining professional motivations

Different outlines of history suggest that different interpretations of the motives of educators are not new. But this does not imply that negative views of professional motivation are unworthy of serious consideration in the present day. The view that professionals are motivated by self-interest can be seen as a counter-weight to the uncritical assumption that every professional, all the time, and in every circumstance, acts with the sole interest of the special child in mind. But,while few professionals are selfless saints, perhaps not all are abject sinners.

Certainly, professionals who work with special children depend for their livelihood on the continued identification of, and the development of, provision for these children. However, fire officers depend for their existence on fires, but this does not inevitably lead to the suspicion that they are clandestine arsonists. The fact that professionals make their living supporting (as they might think) special children does not, of itself, necessarily reveal their intentions or give cause to impugn their motives.

Nonetheless, on a case-by-case basis, there seems nothing wrong with considering the motives of special educators. Nor does there appear anything amiss with examining whether their views and actions are always in the best interests of special children. This is not always straightforward, however. It is sometimes suggested that it would be a positive development for all special children to be educated with other children in mainstream schools. There might be professional resistance to changing the organization of schools that would be required to provide for all pupils (Skrtic, 1991, 1995). If so, it might be an example of professional self-interest coming before what is best for special children, indeed all children.

What is not clear in such debates, however, is whether the underlying premise is correct, that it is inevitably better for all special children to be educated in mainstream. Consequently, it is difficult to determine whether motivations behind resistance to such ideas are predominantly to do with vested professional interests or the best interests of children. Those who argue for mainstreaming may well take the view that professional self-interest is predominant. Those who maintain that special schools and other forms of separate provision have an important place may well take a more positive view of professional motivation.

Professional isolationism

As already indicated, some commentators suggest that special education has been influenced by professional vested interests (Tomlinson, 1982, passim). Professional isolation may be related to this. Even if it is not, it can be argued that, where professional isolationism prevails, it is not in the best interests of special children. Isolationism is likely to engender fragmentation of the service provided for special children and their parents. It can lead to duplication of effort as different professionals tackle the same issue, unaware that other colleagues are trying to deal with it too.

On the other hand, isolationism can produce gaps in provision and, in dealing with day-to-day matters, as different professionals believe, incorrectly, that someone else is dealing with a task. Frustration, lower job satisfaction, mistrust and exhaustion can result. More importantly, where there is isolationism, families do not receive the seamless service they should. The incentive for professionals to work closely together is clearly apparent.

The converse of professional isolationism is close joint professional working. Exploring multidisciplinary working to support special children, Lacey (2000, p. 157) noted that there have been 'several decades of exhortations and initiatives in multidisciplinary and multi-agency working', but that, despite some good practice, there continue to be 'many reports of poor or non-existent joint work between agencies'.

In the United Kingdom, speech and language therapy provision has long been an area where joint working has been problematic. While health services held prime responsibility for speech and language therapy, the 'ultimate' responsibility was with the local education authority. The slow recognition that something needed doing about this anomaly, it has been argued, is related to lack of cooperation at national level (Dessent, 1996). Legislation in 1999 (The Health Act 1999 sections 29–31), enabling partnership arrangements between health bodies and local authorities, seemed to be a step in the right direction.

It is crucial that professionals work with each other and with parents for special children.

But the different training, background, salary, roles and aims of different professions add to the challenge to work coherently. Sometimes the range of professionals involved is daunting (Farrell, 2006a, p. 102).

The assessment of a child who is deafblind will involve contributions from the child and his parents. But it may also include contributions from an audiologist (an audiological scientist trained to perform hearing assessments) and an ophthalmologist (a medical doctor specializing in the diagnosis and treatment of eye diseases), a speech-language pathologist/therapist, a physiotherapist, occupational therapist, a school/ educational psychologist and others.

Longer term, professionals involved with a child who is deafblind and his parents may include: specialist teacher; other teachers; home health visitor; general practitioner/general medical doctor; ear, nose and throat specialist; ophthalmologist; orthoptist (a technician providing exercises aimed at restoring or developing the coordination of the eye system); a technician dealing with hearing aids; audiologist; speech and language pathologist/therapist; occupational therapist; social worker; and school psychologist/educational psychologist.

Several of the particular personnel with whom the child and parent have contact with over the years may move on, making the number of people involved even greater.

It is therefore crucial that the school draws together information and advice from these many sources and uses it to make educational and other judgements about what will enable the child to learn and develop best (Farrell, 2008a, chapter 7).

For a child with traumatic brain injury rehabilitation (restoring previously acquired abilities that have been lost) begins in the intensive care unit and continues for as long as necessary. The initial team may include: physician, nurse, nutritionist or dietician, psychologist, speech-language pathologist/therapist, teacher, occupational therapist, physical therapist/physiotherapist, swallowing therapist (perhaps a speech pathologist or occupational therapist), social worker and recreational therapist. As the child makes progress, the team tends to become smaller, for example: a physician, teacher, psychologist and social worker (Farrell, 2008a, chapter 10).

Yet despite these challenges, certain strategies can improve partnership. The team will need to be as small as possible to achieve the required outcomes. The gradual reducing of the traumatic brain injury team indicates how this can be achieved. Team coordinators with clearly defined roles can help produce the best results from the efforts of the whole group.

Where the purpose of multi professional working is clear, there is better chance of the purpose being fulfilled and greater motivation for professionals to see the child's progress. Teams working on Individual Education Plans/Programmes have such a shared purpose and a clear outcome. In the United States of America, for example, the IEP committee may include a special education teacher, a regular classroom teacher, the child's parents, a parent representative, a school psychologist (to help among other things interpret any assessments) and a school system representative. There may be others with specialist knowledge of the child. The committee has a specific task of establishing the disability classification and the suitable placement. They determine the appropriate services and write the IEP.

In the United States of America, an example of joint working with a clear purpose is that between the classroom teacher and an 'adapted physical education' teacher. The adapted physical education teacher concentrates on fundamental motor skills and physical performance of individual pupils (Gabbard et al., 1994). The classroom teacher and the adapted physical education teacher can work productively together to develop and teach programmes of physical education as well as leisure and recreation.

This may be to help include pupils with developmental coordination disorder or those with health or orthopaedic impairments.

Joint professional training for aspects of work that have shared responsibilities make a valuable contribution. This naturally requires careful planning and preferably prior consultation with a representative sample of likely delegates to ensure the programme covers what different professionals require. Joint presentations, followed by opportunities for groups to discuss, can be helpful. The discussion groups can ensure a cross-section of the different professional groups that are attending. There may also be single professional group discussions to explore very particular implications for one profession with some form of plenary session to bring together different perspectives.

There are good examples of multidisciplinary working involving special schools. These include where many professionals work with the school's pupils and others using the special school as their physical base. Rectory Paddock School and Research Centre (www.rectorypaddock.bromley.sch.uk), a special school in Kent, England carries out multidisciplinary, dynamic child led assessments. In these assessments, a music therapist, a speech and language therapist and a physiotherapist/physical therapist work contemporaneously. This may be used to build up a picture of a child's opportunities, means and motivation to communicate (Farrell, 2006a, p. 103).

At the National Centre for Young People with Epilepsy, in Surrey, England (www.ncype.org.uk), where part of the provision is a special school, a multi-professional assessment service is offered to young people across the United Kingdom. A 3-day diagnostic assessment involves recording brain activity, and includes contributions of nursing and psychological staff (Farrell, 2008a, especially p. 87 and also pp. 86–98).

Professional isolation of another kind, associated with limited awareness of cultural influences, can also lead to distortions. Cross-cultural practice in various professions can be challenging. Looking at the example of Indian cultural influences, it is suggested that conceptualizations of childhood shape the experiences and developments of a child's emotional and recreational repertoires. In cross-cultural practice, child psychiatrists and others are recommended to retain curiosity and humility when coming into contact with other world views (Banhatti et al., 2006, pp. 67–85).

The increase in the use of anti-depressants for children, it has been maintained, is influenced by the development of a 'medicalized notion' of childhood depression. This, it is argued, might be better understood as unhappiness relating to 'cultural dynamics', such as the blurring of boundaries between conceptions of childhood and adulthood (Timimi, 2006, pp. 192–205).

Perhaps it is better if such views are not polarized. Rather like the potentially unhelpful juxtaposition of a supposed individual perspective and a social model view, dichotomy can conceal the complexities of a situation. Examining, in a particular instance, the likely contribution of cultural and medical influences seems one way forward. Such issues lead to a broader consideration of the possible overuse of medication, the subject of the next section.

Overuse of medication

Concerns are sometimes expressed that aspects of special education are too readily seen in a medical light when this may not be the only, or even the best, perspective. This is considered in the chapter 'Sociological criticisms' in relation to a supposed medical or individual model and other alternative perspectives. The present section focuses on the worry that medication may be used when it may not be the best intervention.

The relationship between medical doctors and pharmaceutical companies is seen as sometimes problematic (Jureidini and Mansfield, 2006, pp. 29–39). Worries are expressed where doctors are invited by pharmaceutical companies to attend all-expenses paid seminars at popular vacation sites and subsequently increase their prescribing of the promoted drugs (Orlowski and Wateska, 1992). It has also been reported that pharmaceutical companies have been selective in their publication of favourable research on the use of antidepressants with children (Editorial, *Lancet*, 2004).

It is maintained that '. . . anti-depressant medications have minimal to no effectiveness in childhood depression beyond a placebo effect' (Garland, 2004). Yet American data indicate the prevalence of the use of anti-depressants for children increased from 1.6% to 2.4% from 1998 to 2002 (Delate *et al.*, 2002). More needs to be done, it has been argued, to gain a clearer view of the benefits and harms of drug treatment. An important contribution may be combining the knowledge of randomized trials with pharmacological information from observational studies (Editorial, *British Medical Journal*, 2004).

Debates about medication and children often centre on ADHD. Psychostimulants are the most commonly prescribed drugs for children with this disorder, the most frequently used being methylphenidate or 'Ritalin' (Swanson *et al.*, 1995). The term ADHD emerged from attempts to describe inattentive, overactive and impulsive behaviour. The American Psychiatric Association (2000, pp. 85–93) definition sets out criteria relating to inattention, hyperactivity and impulsivity.

The question of the possible overuse of such medication is brought into focus by the variation in its use. In the United States of America around 90% of pupils with ADHD receive medication of some kind (Greenhill, 1998), while in the United Kingdom, the estimated figure is about 10% (Munden and Arcelus, 1999) with under 6% of children receiving methylphenidate (Ritalin) (National Institute of Clinical Excellence, 2000).

There are related concerns too about the consistency with which decisions about administering medication are made and other matters. In 1998, a survey investigating the use of stimulants in public elementary schools in Laval, Quebec, Canada (Cohen *et al.*, 1999) found that 2% of girls and 6% of boys were taking prescribed stimulants. Discussions were held with five small groups totalling 29 participants: parents, teachers, psychosocial practitioners and physicians. These suggested, '. . . a poorly controlled process of assessment, intervention and follow-up, lacking *explicit* guiding or consensual principles' (Cohen, 2006, p. 151, italics in original). Furthermore, possible side effects for stimulant treatment include loss of appetite, insomnia, changes in mood, nausea and vomiting, and suppression of growth (Fonagy *et al.*, 2005, p. 201). (Please see further discussion in Lloyd *et al.*, 2006.)

The criticism that professionals and others may see a child in medical terms and miss a wider picture is well made. Clearly, professionals always need to keep in mind the particular strengths and limitations of whatever perspective they take. This applies, in fact, not just to a medical standpoint, but also to other perspectives that take a predominantly individual view of disabilities and disorders. These might include perspectives that are: behavioural and observational, neuropsychological, psycholinguistic, psychotherapeutic or developmental. It also applies to other approaches, such as sociological ones. Such standpoints, at their most useful, are temporary ways of looking at evidence that might be used to help the child before returning to the broader conception of the child as a whole.

Turning to the particular issue of the use of medication, any concerns can be balanced against apparent benefits. The example of attention deficit hyperactivity disorder may be taken again. Psychostimulants have been demonstrated to be effective in controlling hyperactive and aggressive behaviour in children with ADHD. The beneficial effects of stimulants for inattention, hyperactivity and impulsivity, at least in the short term, have been confirmed in more than 100 trials. (Please see Fonagy *et al.*, 2002, p. 202, and 199–217 for reviews.) Nevertheless, clear parameters are vital for the use of medication. Stimulant treatment should start with a below optimal dose to reduce the risk of side effects, and as the dose is gradually increased, the effect is monitored both for the drug's effectiveness and for any unwanted reactions (ibid. p. 200).

Members of school staff working with special children who are administered medication need to be aware of the expected effects of the medication. This helps them contribute to an assessment of its effectiveness. If the expectation of administering psychostimulants to a child with ADHD is to improve his ability to concentrate and to focus attention, monitoring needs to establish whether this is happening. At the same time, staff need to be conversant with possible side effects of the medication so that they are part of the monitoring of its safety and effectiveness. This will require initial training, further training to ensure procedures are up to date and on-going support and evaluation.

School staff will liaise with parents and others to ensure they have a clear overall picture of the effects of the medication. This is complicated where medication may be used in combination with other approaches such as behavioural interventions. Then, it is not always possible to ascribe the proportionate contribution to any improvements to one or the other for individual children.

Conclusion

Debates about professional self-interest are not settled by reference to historical examples, as these are conflicting. Sweeping negative generalizations about professional self-interest may be unfair. But neither is it realistic to expect every professional decision to be completely altruistic. Resisting professional isolationism is a continuing challenge and there are examples of good joint working in settings where professionals work face to face on work with specified outcomes. Cross-cultural practice is a further challenge to professionals and their developing understanding and skills. Vigilance is appropriate where there is concern about possible over-reliance on medication. The closer liaison of professionals might have the added benefit of enabling strategies to be applied that lead to the avoidance of, or the minimum use of, medication.

Summary statement: distorting factors

Professionals in special education seek to work closely together for the benefit of special children despite differences in training, background, responsibilities, pay and other potentially constraining factors. More could be done to develop agreement on the criteria used to identify and assess different types of disability and disorder. Vigilance is always required that interventions, including the use of medication, are approached critically.

Thinking points

Readers may wish to consider:

* the balance of evidence for and against professional self-interest and isolationism in coming to a view about the possible motives and contribution of various professionals;
* a range of suitable responses and safeguards possible where there is concern that there may be over-reliance on medication for children;
* other factors that might lead to possible distortions in understanding of special education such as different cultural perspectives.

Key text

Farrell, M. (2009a) *Foundations of Special Education: An Introduction.* New York and London, Wiley. This illustrates special education's diverse disciplines and professional perspectives: legal/typological, terminological, social, medical, neuropsychological, psychotherapeutic, behavioural/observational, developmental, psycholinguistic, technological and pedagogical.

Further reading

Lloyd, G., Stead, J. and Cohen, D. (eds) (2006) *Critical New Perspectives on ADHD.* New York, Routledge.

This relates some of the concerns discussed in the present chapter to the area of attention deficit hyperactivity disorder. There are also chapters questioning the rigour or lack of it with which attention deficit hyperactivity disorder is assessed.

Timimi, S. and Maitra, B. (eds) (2006) *Critical Voices in Child and Adolescent Mental Health*. London, Free Association Books.

Contributors from the field of child and adolescent psychiatry criticize aspects current theory and practice, examining the influence of drug companies, the role of diet and other factors. Several chapters focus on issues relating to attention deficit hyperactivity disorder.

Brantlinger, E. A. (ed.) (2006) *Who Benefits from Special Education? Remediating (Fixing) Other People's Children*. Mahwah, NJ, Lawrence Erlbaum Associated.

Chapter 9 focuses on high stakes testing and hierarchical structures. Chapter 10 draws together some of the threads of earlier chapters.

Chapter 10

Lack of distinctive provision

What is it about 'special' education that distinguishes it from the general education provided for all children? Earlier, in considering the broader topic of provision in the 'Introduction' chapter, it was suggested that aspects of special educational provision are: curriculum, pedagogy, organization of the school and classroom, resources and therapy.

In this context, the present chapter concerns the question of whether there is a special provision for special children. It first examines whether there is distinctive pedagogy and then whether there is a distinctive curriculum. The chapter next considers profiles of distinctive provision for different types of disability and disorder for other aspects of provision.

The view that there is no distinctive provision

Provision for children with disabilities and disorders may be taken to include pedagogy, curriculum and assessment, school and classroom organization, resources and therapy (Farrell, 2008a, passim). The view that there is no distinctive provision for special children implies that there is no requirement or justification for special education. If there is no distinctive provision for children with a disability or disorder, this can be for two reasons. The first is that all children benefit from the same provision. The second reason for having no distinctive provision would be if all children required individual provision because they have predominantly individual needs.

If special education is no different to education for all children, there can be no point in providing it. Indeed, such a view suggests that it may be misguided even to consider children with disabilities and disorders as 'special' at all. Such a position supports inclusion in two senses.

Firstly, it implies that children with disabilities and disorders who are already educated in the mainstream school should receive essentially the same provision as everyone else in mainstream classrooms. If provision for these children is not distinctive, there can be no grounds for any differences in their education. This would suggest that any organizational groupings that presumably enabled different education to take place would be unnecessary. There would be no reason for resource rooms, banding, separate classes or units. Secondly, the position that there is no distinctive provision supports mainstreaming because there can be no argument for separate special schools if provision for all children is essentially the same.

Similarly, if all children require individual provision, there is no case for considering separate provision for children with disabilities or disorders, as they too require individual provision just as does every child. This individual provision can be provided just as easily in one setting as another and there is no justification for grouping children together according to types of disabilities and disorders. For example, there would be no reason for grouping together children with autism because these children would all require individual provision, just as would other children who do not have autism.

The converse also holds. If there is distinctive provision for children with disabilities and disorders, then it can be argued that this limits the extent that inclusion can be meaningful or practicable. If provision that works with a special child is different from that of other children, then there is an argument for separate elements of education that might best take place in separate settings in mainstream schools, or in special schools. It will be seen therefore that arguing that there is no distinctive provision is a central plank of arguments for inclusion.

Is there distinctive pedagogy?

It has been maintained that there is no distinctive pedagogy for special children. More accurately, it has been intimated there are no distinctive pedagogic principles for these children. It may be suggested that what appears to be special pedagogy is simply more intensive versions of how all children are taught. Because of this, it is unnecessary to teach special children separately from others. In fact, they are not 'special' in the sense of requiring anything different to other children.

Lewis and Norwich (2005) delineate ways in which children may be considered to have various needs. These are:

- needs common to all learners
- needs unique to themselves (a unique differences position), and
- needs that may be shared by an identified sub group such as those with a disability or disorder (a general differences position).

Regarding needs common to all learners, it is suggested that this relates to common strategies. Pedagogy in special education may emphasize an approach used also with children who do not have a disorder or disability. For example, pupils with mild cognitive impairment might be taught lessons at a slower pace than peers. But other children who do not have mild cognitive impairment may, for a range of reasons, be taught at a slower pace than is typical.

Also, teaching that appears qualitatively different for special pupils may not be so. It may be only 'more intensive and explicit teaching', representing the 'greater degree of adaptations' to common teaching approaches used with all children (Lewis and Norwich, 2005, pp. 5–6). However, teaching 'geared to pupils with learning difficulties might be inappropriate for average or high attaining pupils' (ibid. p. 6).

In the general difference position, group specific needs of pupils with disabilities or disorders are foregrounded. Nevertheless, needs common to all learners, and needs unique to individual learners, remain important.

The unique difference position emphasizes differences unique to a particular child, de-emphasizes common pedagogic needs and rejects the existence of group specific needs. Learners do have needs common to all children, but they are regarded as also being uniquely different. Differences between individuals are accommodated in terms of personal uniqueness and the dependence of these differences on the social context. (This relates to the strong social view of disability that it is predominantly a socially created phenomenon.) Common pedagogic needs are approached through general principles that enable individual variations to be possible within a common framework (Lewis and Norwich, 2005, pp. 3–4).

Focusing on two positions relating to difference (the general difference position and the unique difference position), Lewis and Norwich (2005) question the usefulness of some groupings of pupils with disabilities or disorders regarding 'pedagogic *principles*' (ibid. p. 216, italics added).

In Lewis and Norwich's edited volume, different contributors considered whether differences between learners, according to disability and disorder, could be identified and linked with a learner's needs for differential teaching. An individual differences position (rejecting group specific differences) was preferred for six types of disability and disorder: deafblindness; severe to moderate cognitive impairment/severe learning difficulty; communication disorders/speech, language and communication needs; dyslexia/reading disorder; social, emotional and behavioural difficulties; and moderate learning difficulties/mild cognitive impairment (pp. 215–216). The editors conclude, 'the traditional special needs categories . . . have limited usefulness in the context of planning, or monitoring, teaching and learning in most areas' (p. 220).

The claim that special needs categories have limited usefulness because they do not support distinctive pedagogy may be a little premature. Several of Lewis and Norwich's (2005) contributors recognized a general differences position (acknowledging group specific differences). This applied to five types of disability and disorder: autistic spectrum disorder, attention deficit hyperactivity disorder, deafness, visual impairment and profound and multiple learning difficulties/profound cognitive impairment. 'Down syndrome' and 'low attainment', not distinctively identified in American or English special education classifications, were also considered. Leaving these two areas aside, a general difference position was supported for five of the eleven disabilities and disorders often considered in classifications.

But even this may not give a full enough picture. It is hardly surprising that a group difference position was not held for the broad and amorphous grouping of, 'behavioural, emotional and social difficulties'. Behavioural, emotional and social difficulties include disruptive behaviour disorders (such as conduct disorder), anxiety and depression. A case can be made for a group difference position for pedagogy for conduct disorder. (Distinctive provision for anxiety disorders and for depressive disorders involves therapy and aspects of the curriculum.)

For adolescents with conduct disorder, various interventions may be used. Among school-based interventions, Gang Resistance Education Training has shown significant effects (Esbensen and Osgood, 1999). Law enforcement officers taught a 9-week curriculum to middle school students that included exercises and interactive approaches intended to underline the consequences of gang violence. Activities taught the skills of goal setting, conflict resolution and standing up to peer pressure. Participating students had lower levels of self-reported delinquency and gang membership than a comparison group. School is an important setting for programmes for conduct disorder and delinquency. School-based mental health resources may also be used to modify the school environment to change characteristics associated with delinquency (Fonagy *et al.*, 2002, p. 171).

In Gang Resistance Education Training, the pedagogy includes exercises and interactive approaches, skills of goal setting, conflict resolution and resisting peer pressure. Importantly, these are combined with a particular curriculum and are delivered by people who would be expected by students to have specialist knowledge of the effects on young people of participating in gangs. The combination of these aspects is likely to have influenced the positive outcomes. However, it can be argued that the pedagogy in the context of the curriculum and teachers is distinctive.

Whatever the views about different types of disability and disorder and distinctive pedagogy, it is clear there is a strong case to be made for such distinctive pedagogic approaches for many types of disability and disorder. However, common needs and unique needs are also considered in developing pedagogy. For children with disabilities or disorders, some approaches may be common to all children, some especially effective with children with the disorder, and some approaches for particular children with the disorder that may be individual to them.

Is there a distinctive curriculum?

It is sometimes argued that there should be no distinctive curriculum for special pupils. This is rather different to claims about there being no distinctive pedagogy. The former seek to drill down to principles of teaching to show that these are the same for all pupils (Lewis and Norwich, 2005). But arguments about the curriculum tend to suggest that any distinctive curriculum is unnecessary and potentially segregating. It is perfectly feasible and preferable if it is suggested to develop a curriculum that is for all pupils including, of course, those with disabilities and disorders. The claim is not so much that there is no distinctive curriculum, but more that there should not be.

Instead, the curriculum should be adapted as a broadly based curriculum for all pupils. Participation and progress would be valued, not only attainment. Staff are encouraged not to see learning difficulty within a pupil, but to re-examine the curriculum. The task is not to remediate pupil weakness, but to adapt the presentation of the curriculum including its planning and the way work is pitched for different pupils.

A school presented as a case study by Skidmore (2004, p. 59) uses the term 'atypical pupils who challenge the curriculum' rather than, for example, 'pupils with disabilities and disorders'. This is a version of a social view of disability and disorder, which places the sole responsibility on the teacher to remove supposed barriers.

It could be argued that such an implied position takes insufficient account of the material reality of the disorder and disability. Curriculum development relates also to adapting pedagogy as necessary. Further training of teachers is advocated to help them develop the skills necessary to plan and deliver the curriculum that is more responsive to all pupils. These points and others relating to school ethos, management implications, pedagogy and values are well summarized in the context of describing a dominant discourse of inclusion in a case study school by Skidmore (2004, pp. 62–63).

The points about widening the reach of a mainstream school curriculum are important. These can be tackled at the planning stage of the curriculum for different subjects or areas of the curriculum. Teachers, working in collaboration with support staff who have particular knowledge of special pupils, can achieve this. Such support for the subject teacher or classroom teacher may take the form of enabling the teacher rather than working directly with the pupil.

However, the question arises about whether there are reasonable limits to what can be expected of curriculum flexibility and teacher adaptability. It is around this area that the debate arises about whether a position is reached where there is a case for a distinctive curriculum for some pupils.

When one begins to examine reasons why atypical pupils 'challenge the curriculum', the challenges arise for different reasons. Some of these relate to disabilities and disorders. One could perhaps try to avoid recognizing this and speak of pupil diversity. But this would miss the point that some pupils do not progress at the same rate as other 'typical' pupils and that there are reasons for this that may not be all to do with the curriculum not being flexible enough.

An example may be taken of cognitive impairment. 'Mild mental retardation' is associated with an intelligence quotient (IQ) range of 50/55 to 70. The diagnostic criteria for mental retardation also include 'co current deficits or impairments in present adaptive functioning . . . in at least two of: communication, self-care, home living, social/interpersonal skills, use of community resources, self-direction, functional academic skills, work, leisure, health and safety' (American Psychiatric Association, 2000, pp. 42, 49). Children with mild mental retardation tend to 'develop social and communication skills during the pre-school years (ages 0 to 5 years)' (p. 43). By the late teens, they can acquire academic skills up to about sixth grade level.

In England, the broadly equivalent category is 'moderate learning difficulties'. Government guidance states that these pupils 'will have attainments well below expected levels in all or most areas of the curriculum, despite appropriate interventions. Their needs will *not* be able to be met by normal differentiation and the flexibilities of the National Curriculum' (DfES, 2005, p. 6, italics added). Attainments are low 'despite appropriate interventions' presumably because of the child's 'difficulty' in 'acquiring basic literacy and numeracy skills and in understanding concepts'.

This suggests that, in most areas of the curriculum, an older pupil with mild cognitive impairment would be working at a level that is typical of a pupil about 4 or 5 years younger. The 'normal flexibilities' of the English National Curriculum, and the teacher pitching work at different levels for different attainment, will not meet the 'needs' of these pupils.

Critics may object to curricula that get increasingly difficult. Negatively intended expressions such as 'technicist' are sometimes used. There are complaints about a standards agenda as if schools should not be about learning things and showing that you have learned them, but should be about being included. But critics tend not to make explicit what planning would enable a pupil who is working at such a different level to others to participate in the same learning as all pupils. If this were at all feasible, there would be no age-grouped classes in schools. Pupils of 10 years old and pupils aged 15 years would be educated together, because the teacher would be able to plan the curriculum to enable all to participate and progress equally well. The rarity of such family grouping might give pause to advocates of this wide curriculum.

The range becomes even wider if one considers pupils with moderate to severe cognitive impairments, or pupils with profound cognitive impairment. For example, a curriculum for pupils with profound cognitive impairment is informed by early infant development and integrates therapy and care. It has very small steps of assessment reflecting the pupils' levels of attainment. Pupils' responses may not necessarily reflect 'vertical', progress, but also experiences and reactions to these.

Concerning children with hearing impairment, curriculum content and related assessment are influenced by whether oral, sign bilingual and total communication methods predominate. For children with visual impairment, the curriculum balance emphasizes the development and use of tactile, mobility and orientation skills and knowledge. Regarding children who are deafblind, the curriculum highlights communication, and cross-curricular audits of skills and understanding may be used.

Distinctive aspects of the curriculum may be identified in relation to different types of disability and disorder. These include disruptive behaviour disorders, anxiety disorders, depressive disorders, and attention deficit hyperactivity disorder. For children with communication disorders of speech, grammar, comprehension, semantics and pragmatics, the content and balance of the curriculum emphasizes communication and its support with respect to the difficulty concerned. Regarding autism, curriculum content and balance emphasizes communication, interaction and social skills. (For fuller details, please see Farrell, 2008a, passim.)

The curriculum may be modified in terms of level and content as for pupils with cognitive impairment. Particular areas or subjects of the curriculum may be planned at a lower than age typical level, where there are difficulties with certain areas such as mathematics. Within subjects and areas of the curriculum, certain threads may be taught at lower than age typical levels, for example, writing. Aspects of the curriculum may be emphasized, such as communication, numeracy, mobility or social development by increasing time allocated to these areas. Cross-curricular planning helps ensure many aspects of the curriculum are closely related to emphasized areas so that they are regularly highlighted in different contexts. Assessment is made in small steps as necessary to recognize progress in areas of difficulty.

Wider issues of provision: resources, therapy and organization

Resources

The term 'resources' is used in this chapter quite broadly. Resources vary in their nature and use according to the type of disability or disorder. For some speech disorders, computer aided communication may be necessary as an alternative or augmentation to speech. This can include a device which, when pressed, plays a simple pre recorded message such as 'good morning' or 'thank you'. It can include very sophisticated computer hardware and software enabling the user to program his original communications by typing them before playing a voice synthesizer to convey the spoken message to others.

For disorder of written expression, computer software is used for essay structure and other aspects of writing. The aim in these circumstances is to provide scaffolding for the pupil so that he can produce suitable work. At the same time, the intention is that the computer-provided support will gradually be internalized by the learner, who will gradually acquire the knowledge and skills to produce written work unaided.

Visual impairment may require low vision devices and lighting, Braille or Moon materials, and computer technology. For children who are deafblind, tactile maps and clues in rooms and corridors can help mobility.

For autism, resources include visual timetables and other materials emphasizing visual clues. These are intended to make the often confusing world of a child with autism more predictable and manageable. Seeing on a visual timetable what is going to happen on a particular morning appears to be more reassuring because it is permanently available. It tends to avoid the child asking over and over for reassurance what the next lesson will be.

A pupil with reading disorder may benefit from reading materials, particularly supporting the development of phonics and computer programs to aid skills development. This may support and complement the work of a speech-language pathologist/therapist on blending and segmenting sound. The computer software may help the pupil link these sounds with the marks that represent text, so they can be linked for reading.

Furniture, aids to movement and other devises are all part of the resources that may be used. Children with orthopaedic impairment need to be correctly positioned, and furniture takes account of pupil's stature and the need for good posture and support. Hoists, assistive walking devices or manual or powered wheelchairs may be used. Separate rooms are provided for personal care procedures and toilets adapted. Work surface can be modified and devices used to help hold objects in one place, and enable the pupil to manipulate items.

Standing aids may assist a child with congenital heart defect, where lessons require long periods of standing. In a school building with stairs, the school may ensure that the classroom and other facilities are on the lower floor or minimize the necessity of stair climbing. Alternatively, a lift may be used. For children with traumatic brain injury, resources may include adaptive equipment to help functioning, such as a wheel-chair, and environmental modifications. Technology may be used to help manual dexterity. (For further examples, please see Farrell, 2008a, passim.)

Therapy

Therapy is perhaps most obviously connected with behavioural and emotional disturbances. Generalized anxiety disorder provision includes cognitive-behavioural therapy (Toren *et al.*, 2000; Kendall *et al.*, 2003, pp. 81–100) and focal psychodynamic psychotherapy (Muratori *et al.*, 2002). For obsessive-compulsive disorder, provision includes medication (Riddle *et al.*, 2001) and cognitive-behavioural therapy (Franklin *et al.*, 1998). Specific and social phobias respond to behavioural interventions (Ollendick and King, 1998, for a review) and cognitive-behavioural therapy (King *et al.*, 2001). For separation anxiety disorder, group cognitive-behavioural therapy has been used (Toren *et al.*, 2000).

Nevertheless, therapy is used with many other types of disability and disorder. With regard to children with speech disorders, speech and language therapy is provided. For a child with disorders of grammar, comprehension, semantics or pragmatics, speech and language therapy is provided as necessary. Regarding traumatic brain injury, the speech-language pathologist/therapist has an important role in assessments. This draws on standardized assessments and observations of the child, interviews with parents and teacher, or curriculum-based language assessment.

Therapy is provided for children with profound cognitive impairment, and for some with moderate to severe cognitive impairment. It is offered for children with mild cognitive impairment where there are 'additional' disorders of communication, conduct, anxiety or depression (Farrell, 2008a, chapters 2, 3 and 4). Physical therapy may be provided for a child with developmental coordination disorder. For children with orthopaedic impairments, medical practitioners, physiotherapists, occupational therapists, prosthetists and others may contribute. (For further discussion of these and therapy in connection with other types of disability and disorder, please see Farrell, 2008a, passim.)

Organization

Organization as it concerns provision for special children relates to school and class-room organization. Organizational aspects also vary with different types of disability and disorder.

For a pupil with profound cognitive impairment, organizational arrangements may include room management/responsive environment (Ware, 2003). This essentially involves ensuring staff roles are clear and that members of staff are fully deployed to make sure that the smallest response from a pupil receives recognition.

The classrooms for children with visual impairment can be organized to optimize hearing clues. This does not imply that the fullest use is not made of any residual vision or that tactile methods are not fully used as suitable. But the long-range sense of hearing is optimized to provide the child with useful information about the environment. The child with visual impairment should be able to hear contributions from other class members. The classroom can be arranged so that there are hearing clues that people are moving towards him or away from him (which is more difficult with carpeted floors and soft shoes).

Similarly, for pupils with hearing impairment, the classroom can be organized to make the best of visual clues. Where signing is used, the pupils will be seated so that all contributions from others can be seen. For lip reading and signed, assisted English, the child needs to see the person who is communicating.

Turning to children with orthopaedic impairments, the school may adopt flexible arrival and departure times for lessons. If the pupil requires adult oversight of movement between lessons, and he leaves with other pupils, the adult can keep at a distance that does not inhibit the pupil's social contact with peers. Outside the classroom, and where there is support in lessons, the level of supervision necessary for recess times will balance safety with encouraging socialization and independence. Flexible arrangements for pupil absences can include home tuition and e-mailed work to support home study (Farrell, 2008a, chapter 8). (For organizational implications for other types of disabilities and disorders, please see Farrell, 2008a, passim.)

Conclusion

For different types of disability and disorder, it is possible to identify a profile of provision that is distinctive in terms of the curriculum, pedagogy, resources, school and classroom organization and therapy.

Summary statement: distinctive provision

Different types of disability and disorder can be associated with distinctive profiles of curriculum, pedagogy, resources, school and classroom organization and therapy.

Thinking points

Readers may wish to consider:

- the extent to which pedagogy, curriculum and assessment, resources, therapy and school and classroom organization capture the essential elements of school provision;
- the varying degrees to which, for each type of disability and disorder, provision can be considered distinctive.

Key text

Farrell, M. (2008a) *Educating Special Children: An Introduction to Provision for Pupils with Disabilities and Disorders*. New York and London, Routledge.

The book considers: profound, moderate to severe, and mild cognitive impairment; hearing impairment; visual impairment; deafblindness; orthopaedic impairment; health impairments; traumatic brain injury; disruptive behaviour disorders; anxiety disorders and depressive disorders; attention deficit hyperactivity disorder; disorders of speech, grammar and comprehension, and meaning and use; autism; developmental disorder; reading disorder; disorder of written expression; and mathematics disorder. It examines curriculum and assessment, pedagogy, resources, therapy and organization.

Further reading

Farrell, M. (2005a) *The Effective Teacher's Guide to Dyslexia and Other Specific Learning Difficulties*. London, Routledge.

Farrell, M. (2005b) *The Effective Teacher's Guide to Moderate, Severe and Profound Learning Difficulties*. London, Routledge.

Farrell, M. (2005c) *The Effective Teacher's Guide to Autism and Communication Difficulties*. London, Routledge.

Farrell, M. (2005d) *The Effective Teacher's Guide to Sensory Impairment and Physical Disabilities*. London, Routledge.

Farrell, M. (2005e) *The Effective Teacher's Guide to Behavioural, Emotional and Social Difficulties*. London, Routledge.

This series of books present practical information and guidance on the topics indicated by their titles, largely assuming a United Kingdom context.

Fonagy, P., Target, M., Cottrell, D., Phillips, J. and Kurtz, Z. (2005) *What Works for Whom? A Critical Review of Treatments for Children and Adolescents*. New York, The Guilford Press.

This book presents evidence-based practice for anxiety disorders, depressive disorders, disturbance of conduct, attention deficit hyperactivity disorder, Tourette's disorder, autism, specific development disorders (concerning communication, motor skills, reading, mathematics and writing) and other disorders. It concentrates on psychosocial and pharmacological approaches.

Lewis, A. and Norwich, B. (eds) (2005) *Special Teaching for Special Children? Pedagogies for Inclusion*. Maidenhead, UK, Open University Press.

This edited book comprises the views of specialists as to whether there is a specific pedagogy for different disabilities and disorders. Chapters cover deafness, visual impairment, deafblindness, severe learning difficulties (severe to moderate cognitive impairment), profound and multiple learning difficulties (profound cognitive impairment), communication difficulties, autism, attention deficit hyperactivity disorder, dyslexia, dyspraxia, moderate leaning difficulties (mild cognitive impairment) and social, emotional and behavioural difficulties.

Mitchell, D. (ed.) (2004d) *Special Educational Needs and Inclusive Education: Major Themes in Education, Volume 4: Effective Practices*. London and New York, Routledge Falmer.

A selection of previously published journal articles, some of which concern strategies for particular disabilities and disorders.

Chapter 11

The alternative of inclusion as mainstreaming

The present chapter's consideration of inclusion differs from that of issues previously discussed. Sociological, rights-based and post-modern criticisms and other issues covered in previous chapters constitute direct criticisms of special education. Inclusion, however, is not so much a criticism of special education as a proposed replacement. This chapter considers the nature of inclusion and criticisms of it. Indications of the declining influence of inclusion are identified.

There is some overlap between the present chapter and Chapter 3. The main difference is that the earlier chapter emphasizes special education, supposedly denying rights. The present chapter emphasizes inclusion being presented as an alternative to special education.

What is inclusion?

Inclusion has been described as provision for all students including those with disabilities, giving 'equitable opportunities to receive effective educational services'. This would be in 'age-appropriate classes in neighbourhood school' and would include as necessary, 'supplemental aids and support services' (National Center on Inclusive Education and Restructuring, 1995, p. 6). Antia *et al.* (2002) describe inclusion as involving a student with a disability belonging to, and having full membership of, a regular classroom, in an ordinary school in the local community. Full inclusion implies that all children are educated together in the same mainstream classrooms, following the same curriculum at the same point in time, and experiencing pedagogy essentially the same as other children (see Chapter 9).

Full inclusion would preclude the need for special education. There would be no need for separate provision in special schools or units because all children would be educated in mainstream classes. Also, there would be no need for any of the identification, assessment, classification or distinctive provision associated with special education. This is because nothing different would be provided for children with disabilities and disorders than for other children. They would follow the same curriculum with essentially the same pedagogy. Classroom support and resources might be different, but this would be seen as part of the variation that might be made for any child. Therapy provision is not very often considered in this scenario.

Other definitions of inclusion emphasize participation. Pupils may be educated in a range of settings including special schools, separate units based on a mainstream school campus, part- time support in a resources room or full participation in a mainstream classroom. All these settings would be seen as been equally able to provide inclusive environments. In brief, inclusion may be taken as a euphemism for mainstreaming, or it may be intended as an encouragement to improving pupils' participation in whatever setting they are educated.

Inclusive pedagogy concerns approaches to teaching and learning that emphasize and try to ensure the participation of all pupils. The term reflects the differences found in definitions of inclusion itself. For some, inclusive pedagogy is appropriate for special schools and mainstream schools. For others, it is associated with educating special children in a mainstream classroom and seeking to ensure he takes part as fully as possible.

In the United States of America, 'adapted physical education' (APE) is an individualized programme provided by people who have studied the requirements of physical education instruction for children with disabilities. The APE teacher concentrates on fundamental motor skills and physical performance of individual pupils and may work with pupils for a specified number of hours per week (Gabbard *et al.*, 1994). The classroom teacher and APE teacher work together to develop and teach programmes of physical education as well as leisure and recreation. While some strategies can be effective in encouraging participation, it is not always established if they are effective in enabling a special child to learn and develop better. If this is demonstrated, then of course the pedagogy becomes not just inclusive pedagogy but effective pedagogy.

The criticisms considered in relation to inclusion in this chapter generally concern inclusion as mainstreaming.

Some criticisms of inclusion

Inclusion as a primary aim

The view that inclusion is, or should be, a primary aim of schools is not easy to maintain. Rather too many people think that schools ought to be about education. Parents tend to send their children to school to be educated, not primarily to be included. The prospect of leaving school having learned little and developed less, but being able to claim to have been included does not appeal to many parents or pupils. The primary aim of a hospital is to make people better. The key object of a transport service is to get passengers from A to B on time. The main motive of a fire service is to put out fires. For none of these services can inclusion be the primary aim. If it is, the service runs the risk of sidelining the main reason why it was set up in the first place. So it is with schools. Education is a school's primary purpose, not inclusion (Farrell, 2006a).

Of course, inclusion can be an important secondary aim (Barrow, 2001). To decide whether a child in a mainstream school will benefit from special education is an educational decision. It is based on judgements and evidence that the child will make better progress academically and will develop better personally and socially. Again, the issue of whether this special education is given in part in separate classes is an educational one in the broadest sense. A judgement that a child will be better educated and will develop better in a separate special school is similarly, at heart, an educational one. Once this is agreed in a decision involving the child, parents, teachers and others, then the aim of inclusion in the sense of the fullest participation in whatever setting is suitable can be an important consideration.

Inclusion as liberation from oppression

Inclusion as liberation can only be convincing if it can be demonstrated that special educational provision, including provision in special schools, is constraining or limiting of freedom. Therefore, inclusionists point to the supposed oppressive nature of special education. Oppression has been defined as, 'inhuman or degrading treatment of individuals or groups; prejudicial behaviour acting against the interests of those people who characteristically tend to belong to relatively powerless groups in the social structure' (Thompson, 2001, p. 33).

The pervasiveness of a 'medical model' has been seen as related to the authority and dominance of groups such as medical personnel (Fulcher, 1989). Similarly, it is suggested that the medical and welfare professions as groups 'in power' produce definitions of normality (Abberley, 1989, p. 57). The concept of 'normalization', and practices to which it might lead, has been criticized.

Dominant definitions are said to have 'created a number of *oppressive* practices for disabled people' (Vlachou, 1997, p. 22, italics added). Regarding 'charity images' of disability, some posters suggesting disabled people using wheelchairs need to break free of them when they are a part of the person's daily life, 'impose further *oppression* on disabled people' (Vlachou, 1997, p. 23). A disabled person feeling they have to deny their difference and normalizing their situation while working conditions remain the same leads to the working conditions becoming '*oppressive* for them'. The socio-political effect of normalization on disabled people of creating 'heroic' images, however, 'is even more *oppressive*'. This is partly because such 'heroism' obscures what are argued to be 'the social origins of the *oppression* of disabled people'. The 'external *oppression*' of denying difference to be 'normal' creates, 'another from of *oppression* for disabled people, 'internal *oppression*' (ibid. p. 24, italics added in all quotations).

Reiser and Mason (1992) writing of the experience of disability also suggest that 'internalized *oppression*' would not exist without, 'real external *oppression* which forms part of the social climate in which we exist' (ibid. p. 27, italics added). It has been stated that, 'the idea of special educational needs is one instance of a range of categories which *oppress* disabled people' (Fulcher, 1995, p. 9, italics added).

Such deliberations on normalization as a concept and a process raise some worthwhile points. But any link among special education, labels and external or internal oppression seems wide of the mark for many. Special children and young people and their parents steadfastly seem unable to recognize that they are being degraded and treated inhumanly, as they enjoy activities with their friends and learn and achieve well. Parents and children persist in seeing their special education as liberating rather than oppressive. Being able to learn well and participate with other children and enjoy the experience counts for more than being forced into a mainstream classroom. One person's oppression clearly is another's liberation.

The pursuit of equality of opportunity

The view that a special child would have equality of opportunity for a good education or participation if placed in a mainstream classroom is also difficult to maintain. The approach seemed to repeat arguments regarding other groups deemed to lack equal opportunities, such as different racial groups. A child from an ethnic minority would be expected to have the equal opportunity of a place in a mainstream classroom unless there were reasons prohibiting admission. (For example, the applicant could be a boy and the school could be for girls only.) Regarding ethnicity, there would be no grounds on which he should not be admitted. Once in the school, there would be no grounds for expecting that he would not progress as well as others.

For a special child, the situation may well be different. The child may be entitled to a place in a mainstream classroom and might be offered such a place. But the difference between the levels at which the child is working and that at which others are working may be very wide. The child may have cognitive impairment such that he is attaining at a level typical of a child 5 or 6 years younger than other children in his class. It would impracticable for a typical teacher to teach to that range of attainment. Therefore, being a member of that class group is not the same as having an equal opportunity to learn and participate as other children.

A similar situation may be envisaged for a child with severe autism, conduct disorder and other disabilities and disorders. The child would not be 'included' in any generally accepted meaning of the term, but would simply be physically present in the classroom.

Inclusion as a right

In Scotland, estate owner Charles Fforde is reported to have accused the Scottish Executive of 'breaching his human rights' by abolishing the feudal system (Peterkin, 2004). In England, a retired police officer is stated to be prepared to take to the European Court of Human Rights a claim he should be able to cut down protected trees in his garden blocking his television satellite signal. The complainant considers it a 'basic human right to receive television signals and enjoy watching television' (Sapsted, 2004).

Kundera (1991) argues, 'the more the fight for human rights gains in popularity the more it loses any concrete content'. Everything has become a right. 'The desire for love the right to love' and so on (ibid. p. 154). Glendon (1991) maintains, '. . . there is very little agreement regarding *which* needs, goods, interests, or values should be characterized as "rights", or concerning what should be done when . . . various rights are in tension or collision with one another' (ibid. p. 16, italics in original). Rights rhetoric is bound up with '. . . a near silence concerning responsibility, and a tendency to envision the rights-bearer as a lone autonomous individual' (p. 45).

Glendon's (1991) linking of rights and responsibilities shares common ground with Benn and Peters' (1959, pp. 88–89) perception of the reciprocal nature of rights and duties in which a right implies a correlative duty on others. Rights rhetoric seems to reject the view that a right is a rule-bound normative phenomenon and seems to perceive it as a quality that an individual somehow owns.

As in many other spheres, in special education many supposed rights have been claimed. Among these is the 'right' to be educated in an ordinary school, claimed by those who regard inclusion as synonymous with mainstreaming. Yet this does not prevent others from claiming exactly opposite rights. So parents and children can with equal credibility claim the 'right' to special education in a mainstream school or a special school. The parents of a child who is deaf can claim the right for the child to be educated in a mainstream classroom because he is a member of an oppressed group. They can equally express the right for the child to be educated in a special school where he can learn deaf sign language because he is member of a linguistic minority.

Inclusion as fairness

As suggested in the earlier chapter 'Rights-based criticisms and contested values' in the section on social justice, while inclusion is supposedly informed by the principle of fairness, this means different things to different people. A principle of fairness is that, 'It is morally wrong, in itself, to treat individuals differently without providing relevant reasons for doing so'. However, it has to be clear what the 'relevant reasons' are, as they depend on context and have to be established by independent reasoning. Whether behaviour is 'fair' is determined with reference to other substantive moral values and the facts of a situation. This does not imply that fairness cannot be part of a coherent moral viewpoint (Barrow, 2001, pp. 236–240). However, if taken as a principle of school practice, inclusion can lead to unfairness.

The term 'fairness' may be 'under-extended' when used to argue for the education of special pupils in ordinary schools (Farrell, 2009a, chapter 3). It may be maintained it is not 'fair' to exclude pupils from education in an ordinary school when they do not differ from other children in the school. Here, the concept of 'fairness' is applied with the assumption that there are no relevant differences between pupils with, and without, a disability or disorder. However, the concept of fairness can be extended to apply to the extent to which it is 'fair' to educate pupils in ordinary schools, where there *is* a relevant difference, between pupils with and without disability or disorder.

Recognition that the concept of fairness can be applied to both circumstances may lead to a clearer consideration of issues. These include whether there is any point at which it can be agreed that differences between a special student and a student without a disability or disorder is relevant to the place where the child is predominantly educated. Such differences might include very wide differences in cognitive abilities or behaviour. This makes it possible to examine further issues rather than be deadlocked because of an unacknowledged difference in the use of the concept of 'fairness'.

Lack of empirical evidence to support inclusion

Evidence regarding inclusion is equivocal. Marston (1996) considered pupils with 'mild disabilities'. Comparisons were made between inclusion only, pull-out only, and combined service delivery. Higher increases were found for reading attainment with pupils experiencing the combined service. Manset and Semmel (1997) also looked at pupils with 'mild disabilities'. They reviewed evidence of different levels of progress of pupils on eight model programmes. They conclude, 'Inclusive programming effects are relatively unimpressive for most students with disabilities', especially considering the 'extraordinary resources available to many on these model programmes' (p. 177).

Mills *et al.* (1998) compared the effects of special school, integrated provision and mainstream class. They looked at the progress made by pre-schoolers in verbal and perceptual skills. Higher functioning children benefited more from integrated provision. Lower functioning children gained more from special school or mainstream classroom.

Stanovich *et al.* (1998) studied inclusive classrooms in Canada, finding that pupils with disabilities had lower self-concepts and lower acceptance by peers than 'non-categorized' pupils.

Salend and Duhaney (1999), in a review of the effect of inclusion on students with disabilities, noted that some studies found improved educational outcomes of various kinds, while other studies found the student did not receive specially designed instruction and some did better in traditional special education services.

Analyses have been made of students' perceptions across eight studies. This suggested social benefits accrued to students in a general education setting compared with when they were withdrawn to a resources room. However, students preferred to receive their support in the resource room rather than in their usual classes, believing they were able to concentrate better. Older students also said they learned more (Vaughan and Klinger, 1998). A review of the educational achievement of deaf children found that several studies pointed to higher achievement in mainstream schools. However, many of these studies had not taken into account factors that could distort the findings (Powers *et al.*, 1999).

Peetsma *et al.* (2001) report a study on the academic and psychosocial development of students with mild learning and behavioural difficulties in the Netherlands. After 2 years, the students with difficulties made better progress in mathematics in inclusive settings, but students in special schools made better in school motivation. After 4 years, students in ordinary schools had made better progress in academic performance, but there were no differences in psychosocial development. A qualitative study indicated that students with psychosocial problems made better progress in special settings than in ordinary settings.

Lindsay (2003) reviewing overviews and reviews, concluded, they 'cannot be said to be ringing endorsements' and 'fail to provide clear evidence for the benefits of inclusion' (ibid. p. 6). Kavale and Mosert (2003) in an article entitled 'River of ideology, islands of evidence' speak of 'full inclusion spin' having influence 'disproportionate to its claims for efficacy' (ibid., abstract). They argue caution because, at best, evidence is mixed.

Given this picture, parents may make decisions about what is the best school according to local as well as other factors. A parent with the opportunity to apply for her child to attend a first-rate special school or a second-rate comprehensive school, is unlikely to choose according to ideology. Conversely, where the choice is between a struggling special school, perhaps starved of resources and pupils by an 'inclusive' local authority, and a thriving mainstream school, the parent is likely to choose the latter. These decisions are also influenced by such considerations as the child's age and the type of disability and disorder and its severity.

Where parents have information about local schools, this can inform their decision about whether to apply for a special school place or an ordinary school. In Hampshire, a local authority in England, parents and schools have, for some years, been able to see data showing the progress made by special pupils in mainstream and special settings. These are available for different types of disability and disorder, for example, moderate learning difficulty (mild cognitive impairment). Parents can then make their decision about which school might best suit their child informed by this data. Hampshire supports 38 thriving special schools (Farrell, 2006a, pp. 89–91).

Relationships between criticisms of special education and claims for inclusion

Criticisms of special education can be seen as endorsements of inclusion. The challenge to special education about perspectives wrongly depicts special education as being entrenched in a medical and individual model when it takes account of many perspectives. The idea that inclusion as a standards bearer of the social model, itself flawed, could replace special education has been found wanting.

If rights-based criticisms are correct and the value system of special education is wrong, inclusion is the answer. It responds to the very rights that special education is depicted as denying. But the claim that only inclusionists have values to speak of, and that anything counter to inclusion is unjust, divisive or demeaning, seems increasingly like prejudice.

Post-modern, post-structuralist and hermeneutic approaches may suggest fresh ways of looking at special education and its related disciplines and point to problems with meaning, dichotomous thought and the historical contingency of current arrangements. But attempts to work out any unproblematic implications of these ideas for special education or alternatives have not been forthcoming.

The idea that the knowledge base of special education was limited to a bit of behavioural psychology and scraps of medicine and psychiatry proves equally muddled. The very wide base on which special education draws has always been apparent to those working in the area. Therefore, the alternative of inclusion is not as attractive if special education is not seen as simply in the thrall of an impoverished knowledge base and needing only a bit more common humanity.

From an inclusion perspective, classification would be seen as unnecessary, as there is nothing essentially different to classify. But the idea that classification is, of itself, restrictive and divisive ceases to carry much credibility if classifications are recognized to be about disabilities and disorders and not children. The useful links with evidence-based provision further erode the negative view of classification.

For supporters of inclusion, assessment might be seen as irrelevant and constraining. But claims that assessments, especially those of intelligence, are biologically reductionist were seen to be wide of the mark, even where Nazi Germany was regularly invoked.

If all children were uniformly educated in a mainstream classroom, there would be no need for labelling, which is seen by some inclusionists as purely negative. Yet the positive implications of identification and the deployment of positive labels seem to run counter to this view.

Those wanting to demean special education and phase out special schools might think professionals are out to gain self-aggrandizement. But this seems to jar with the perceptions of parents and children, who daily see professionals going far beyond the call of duty to educate and care for special children.

If inclusionists were correct in their perceptions, it would be recognized that there is no grounds for supposing a special provision for special children. Therefore, there would be no argument for any kind of separate provision. All pupils could, and should, be educated in a mainstream classroom together. However, the suggestion that special educators are doing nothing different to mainstream teachers, because children all learn according to the same principles, does not bear serious scrutiny.

In all of these cases, criticisms are made of special education and an implication is that mainstreaming would be a better alternative. As the preceding chapters have sought to demonstrate, however, none of these criticisms can be sustained. At the same time that criticisms of special education can be seen to be ill informed, it is possible to discern the decline of inclusion as an alternative.

The declining influence of inclusion and related policy changes

Some commentators detect lack of progress towards inclusion. Dyson (2001) suggests there is an 'inclusion backlash' (ibid. p. 26). Allen (2006) refers to 'Frustration with the faltering rate of progress toward full inclusion . . .' (ibid. pp. 27–28). Furthermore, '. . . we continue to mythologize progress towards inclusion' (p. 28). Malign reasons have been suggested. It is said, 'Much of the failure to make progress with inclusion has been recognized as lying with the continued malevolent influence of special needs paradigm, with its medical and charity discourses, and which engenders deficit orientated practices . . .' (p. 28).

England still has a highly respected special school system educating tens of thousands of children (Farrell, 2006a, 2008a), and arguments for inclusion as mainstreaming have less and less influence. There have been periods when government have been confused and sent out mixed messages (Farrell, 2008a, preface pp. xiii–xiv) and, during the period 1997 to 2007, around 9000 special school places were lost (Balchin, 2007, chapter 6). But after over 20 years of arguments about inclusion, a New Labour government report endorsed the work of special schools (Department for Education and Skills, 2003). In evidence to the House of Commons Education and Skills Committee, the minister then responsible for special education stated, the government, 'have no policy whatever, I should stress, of encouraging local authorities to close special schools' (House of Commons Education and Skills Committee, 2006, p. 6).

A Conservative Party commissioned report (Balchin, 2007) has stated that the policy of inclusion has caused 'grievous damage' not only to special children '. . . but to their peers in mainstream education, their teachers and their parents' (ibid. chapter 5). The report calls for a moratorium on the closure of special schools and an exploration of 'how we might recreate the number of places that have been destroyed' (ibid. chapter 6). The shadow education secretary, Michael Gove, stated, 'In the last ten years, the failed ideology of inclusion and the drop in special school places have left the more vulnerable more exposed' (www.publicservice.co.uk/news_story.asp?id=3463).

In the United States of America, the effect of evidence-based practice has led to further questioning of inclusion as mainstreaming. If the evidence has to indicate the academic progress and psychosocial development of pupils, it becomes harder to argue for inclusion as the central value of education.

Conclusion

Inclusion developed as an alternative to special education. However, it has been unable to make meaningful challenges to special education, is weak when it seeks to be a primary aim of schooling, and fails in its guise of offering a way to liberation and equal opportunities. Inclusion is hoist on its own petard when it claims to be a right. This is because it is either rejected as being yet another 'I Want' type of right, or because others decide to create a 'right' to choose special school education. The claim that inclusion is fair is also difficult to sustain. Empirical evidence supporting inclusion is lacking and insufficient note is sometimes taken of possible different implications and outcomes for inclusion with reference to different types of disability and disorder. Where local information is available, this can guide parents to choose the best school for their child.

Special education, unlike inclusion, recognizes education and development as a primary aim of schooling, offers social justice, and its approaches are supported by empirical evidence.

Summary statement

Special education recognizes education and development as primary aims of schooling.

Thinking point

Readers may wish to consider:

*   whether the points examined in this chapter are the main criticisms of inclusion.

Key text

Farrell, M. (2004) *Inclusion at the Crossroads: Concepts and Values in Special Education*. London, David Fulton.
This book looks at various concepts and values in special education including: equality and discrimination, self-interest and cooperativeness, balances of power, representation, rationality and autonomy, and rights and duties, and distinguishing different types of supposed 'need'.

Further reading

Farrell, M. (2008b) *The Special School's Handbook: Key Issues for All*. London, Routledge/National Association for Special Education.
Considers ways special schools might develop and includes many case studies of schools. It considers developing the curriculum and organizational innovations enabling special schools and ordinary schools to work more closely together. It looks at the changing roles of professionals and ways of assessing pupils' progress and development.

Kauffman, J. M. and Hallahan, D. P. (1995) *The Illusion of Full Inclusion: A Comprehensive Critique of a Current Special Education Bandwagon*. Austin, TX, PRO-ED.
A robust criticism of full inclusion, which views it as based more on rhetoric than or research evidence.

Mitchell, D. (ed.) (2004b) *Special Educational Needs and Inclusive Education: Major Themes in Education, Volume 2: Inclusive Education*. London and New York, Routledge Falmer.
This comprises a selection of articles that have previously appeared in various journals. The editor's lucid introduction draws out themes of the concept of inclusion, its origins and rationale, implementation and critiques of inclusion.

Chapter 12

Conclusion

The points raised in the previous chapters concerned:

- sociological criticisms
- rights-based criticisms and contested values
- post-modern criticisms
- concerns about the special education knowledge base
- classification
- assessment
- labelling
- professional limitations
- the question of special provision, and
- calls for inclusion.

In responding to these criticisms, special education has becomes strengthened.

Drawing on the summary statements at the end of previous chapters, a fuller definition and description of special education can be attempted. References in parenthesis after the points indicate chapters from which they derive.

Special education concerns provision, for pupils with disabilities and disorders comprising: curriculum and assessment, pedagogy, school and classroom organization, resources and therapy. It aims to encourage the academic progress and personal and social development of special children (see Chapter 1). It draws on individual, social, organizational and other perspectives to inform understanding and practice (see Chapter 2).

Special education strives for greater equality of outcomes for pupils, respects the voice of parents, children and others connected with special education and is committed to social justice and service to the community (see Chapter 3). Special education draws on evidence-based approaches, professionals seek to be aware of the power and knowledge implications of their roles and efforts are made to elicit and respond to pupil's views and feelings (see Chapter 4).

The knowledge base of special education includes a wide range of disciplines and contributions supplemented by related research and methods informing evidence-based practice. It is tempered by training and professional judgement about what works in day-to-day teaching (see Chapter 5).

Categorical classifications such as 'autism' or 'profound cognitive impairment' can support evidence-related provision, and dimensional classifications such as 'participation restrictions' and 'activity limitations' can enable monitoring of progress of individuals and groups, and inform resource allocation (see Chapter 6). Functional, support-based and other assessments, including assessments of intelligence contribute productively to a fuller picture of a child's abilities and skills (see Chapter 7).

Special educators strive to ensure the positive labelling of children receiving special education, their parents and others working in special education (see Chapter 8). Professionals in special education seek to work closely together for the benefit of special children, despite differences in training, background, responsibilities, pay and other potentially constraining factors. More could be done to develop agreement on the criteria used to identify and assess different types of disability and disorder. Vigilance is always required that interventions, including the use of medication, are approached critically (see Chapter 9).

Different types of disability and disorder can be associated with distinctive profiles of curriculum, pedagogy, resources, school and classroom organization and therapy (see Chapter 10). Special education recognizes education and development as a primary aim of schooling (see Chapter 11).

Some criticisms of special education have been based on misunderstandings or lack of knowledge of contemporary theory and practice. However, the criticisms are sometimes justified and, where this is so, special education is able to respond and modify its approaches. As it has done so, the alternative of inclusion and such influences as social views of 'disability' have diminished in importance while special education has been strengthened.

Thinking points

Readers may wish to consider:

- whether the points examined in the book concern the main criticisms of special education;
- the degree to which the discussion of the book addresses criticisms of special education satisfactorily;
- the extent to which the concluding description of special education captures its remit.

Bibliography

Abberley, P. (1989) 'Disabled people, normality and social work', in Barton, L. (ed.) *Disability and Dependency*. Lewes, UK, The Falmer Press.

Adams, G. L. and Engelmann, S. (1996) *Research on Direct Instruction: 25 Years Beyond DISTAR*. Seattle, WA: Educational Achievement Systems.

Alberto, P. A. and Troutman, A. C. (2005) (7th edition) *Applied Behavioural Analysis for Teachers*. Columbus, OH, Merrill/Prentice Hall.

Algozzine, B. and Ysseldyke, E. (2006b) *Teaching Students with Mental Retardation: A Practical Guide for Teachers*. Thousand Oaks, CA, Corwin Press.

Allen, J. (1996) 'Foucault and special educational needs: a "box of tools" for analysing children's experiences of mainstreaming', *Disability and Society*, **11**(2), 219–33.

Allen, J. (2006) 'Failing to make progress? The aporias of responsible inclusion', in Brantinger, E. A. (ed.) *Who Benefits From Inclusion? Remediating (Fixing) Other People's Children*. Mahwah, NJ and London, Lawrence Erlbaum Associates.

Alston, P. (1984) 'Conjuring up new human rights: a proposal for quality control', *American Journal of International Law*, **78**, 607–21.

American Psychiatric Association (2000) *Diagnostic and Statistical Manual of Mental Disorders Fourth Edition Text Revision*. Washington DC, APA.

American Psychological Association Task Force (1995) *Intelligence: Knowns and Unknowns*. Arlington, VA, APA.

Antia, S. D., Stinson, M. S. and Gaustad, M. G. (2002) 'Developing membership in the education of deaf and hard-of-hearing students in inclusive settings', *Journal of Deaf Studies and Deaf Education*, **7**, 214–29 .

Appleton, R. and Gibbs, J. (1998) *Epilepsy in Childhood and Adolescence*. London, Dunitz.

Balchin, R. (2007) *Commission on Special Needs in Education: The Second Report*. London, CSNE.

Bandman, B. (1973) 'Do children have any natural rights? *Proceedings of the 29th Annual General Meeting of the Philosophy of Education Society*, **2**, 34–42.

Bandura, A. (1977) *Social Learning Theory*. Englewood Cliffs, NJ, Prentice-Hall.

Banhatti, R., Dwivedi, K. and Maitra, B. (2006) 'Childhood: an Indian perspective', in Timimi, S. and Maitra, B. (eds) (2006) *Critical Voices in Child and Adolescent Mental Health*. London, Free Association Books.

Barkley, R. (1997) *ADHD and the Nature of Self Control*. New York, Guilford Press.

Barnes, C. and Mercer, G. (1996) *Exploring the Divide: Illness and Disability*. Leeds, Leeds Disability Press.

Barrow, R. (2001) 'Inclusion vs. fairness', *Journal of Moral Education*, **30**(3), 235–42.

Beaton, A. A. (2004) *Dyslexia, Reading and the Brain: A Sourcebook of Biological and Psychological Research*. London, Psychology Press.

Bebko, J. M., Perry, A. and Bryson, S. (1996) 'Multiple method validation study of Facilitated Communication: II Individual differences and sub group results', *Journal of Autism and Developmental Disorders*, 26(1), 19–42.

Becker, H. (1963) *Outsiders: Studies in the Sociology of Deviance*. Chicago, IL, Chicago University Press.

Beitchman, J. H. and Young, A. R. (1997) 'Learning disorders with a special emphasis on reading disorders: a review of the past ten years', *Journal of the American Academy of Child and Adolescent Psychiatry* 40, 75–82.

Benjamin, S. (2002) *The Micropolitics of Inclusion: An Ethnography*. Buckingham, UK, Open University Press/McGraw-Hill Education.

Benn, S. I. and Peters, R. S. (1959) *Social Principles and the Democratic State*. London, George Allen and Unwin.

Berger, P. L. and Luckmann, T. ([1966]/1975) *The Social Construction of Reality*. Harmondsworth, Penguin Books.

Bernstein, J. H. (2000) 'Developmental neuropsychological assessment', in Yeates, K. O., Ris, M. D. and Taylor, H. G. (eds) *Paediatric Neuropsychology: Research, Theory and Practice*. New York, Guilford Press, pp. 405–38.

Blagg, N. R. and Yule, W. (1984) 'The behavioural treatment of school refusal: a comparative study', *Behaviour Research and Therapy*, 22, 119–27.

Bouchard, T. J., Lykken, D. T., McGue, M., Segal, N. L. and Tellegen, A. (1990) 'Sources of human psychological differences: the Minnesota Study of Twins Reared Apart', *Science*, 250, 223–8.

Brantlinger, E. A. (ed.) (2006) *Who Benefits from Special Education? Remediating (Fixing) Other People's Children*. Mahwah, NJ, Lawrence Erlbaum Associates.

Bromfield, R., Wiz, J. R. and Messer, T. (1986) 'Children's judgements and attributions in response to the mentally retarded label: a developmental approach', *Journal of Abnormal Psychology*, 95, 81–7.

Bury, M. (2000) 'A comment on the ICIDH2', *Disability and Society*, 15(7), 1073–7.

Campbell, J. and Oliver, M. (1996) *Disability Politics: Understanding Our Past, Changing Our Future*. London, Routledge.

Carlson, C. L., Pelham, W. E., Milich, R. and Dixon, J. (1992) 'Single and combined effects of methylphenidate and behaviour therapy on the classroom performance of children with attention deficit hyperactivity disorder', *Journal of Abnormal Child Psychology*, 20, 213–32.

Carr, A. (2006) (2nd edition) *The Handbook of Child and Adolescent Clinical Psychology: A Contextual Approach*. London, Routledge.

Cavanaugh, M. (2002) *Against Equality of Opportunity*. Oxford, Oxford University Press.

Centre for Studies in Inclusive Education (2003) *Reasons Against Segregated Schooling*. Bristol, Centre for Studies in Inclusive Education.

Cohen, D. (2006) 'How does the decision to medicate children arise in cases of ADHD? Views of parents and professionals in Canada', in Lloyd, G., Stead, J. and Cohen, D. (eds) (2006) *Critical New Perspectives in ADHD*. New York, Routledge.

Cohen, D., Clapperton, I., Gref, P., Tremblay, Y. and Cameron, S. (1999) *DAH: Perceptions de acteurs et utilization de psychostimulants*. Laval, QC, Regional Health and Social Services Board of Laval.

Cole, T. (1989) *Apart or A Part? Integration and the Growth of British Special Education*. Milton Keynes, Open University Press.

Corbett, J. (1996) *Bad Mouthing: The Language of Special Needs.* London, Routledge.

Cutting, L. E. and Denckla, M. B. (2003) 'Attention: relationships between Attention-Deficit Hyperactivity Disorder and Learning Disability', in Swanson, H. L., Harris, K. R. and Graham, S. (eds) (2003) *Handbook of Learning Disabilities.* New York, The Guilford Press.

Danermark, B. and Gellerstedt, L. C. (2004) 'Social justice: redistribution and recognition – a non-reductionist perspective on disability', *Disability and Society,* **19**(4), 339–53.

Danforth, S. and Rhodes, W. C. (1997) 'Deconstructing disability: a philosophy for inclusion', *Remedial and Special Education,* **18**, 357–66.

Dawe, A. (1970) 'The two sociologies', *British Journal of Sociology,* **21**, 2.

Delate, T., Gelenberg, A. J., Simmons, V. A. and Motheral, B. R. (2002) 'Trends in the use of anti depressants in a national sample of commercially insured paediatric patients, 1998 to 2002', *Psychiatric Services,* **55**, 387–91.

Department for Education and Skills (2001) *Special Educational Needs Code of Practice.* London, DfES.

Department for Education and Skills (2003) *The Report of the Special Schools Working Group.* London, DfES.

Department for Education and Skills (2005) (2nd edition) *Data Collection by Type of Special Educational Need.* London, DfES.

Derrida, J. ([1967]/1973) *Speech and Phenomena.* Evanston, IL, North Western University Press (translated from the French by D. B. Allison).

Derrida, J. ([1967]/1997) (corrected edition) *Of Grammatology.* Baltimore, Johns Hopkins University (translated from the French by Gayatri Chakravorty Spivak).

Derrida, J. ([various dates and 1967]/1978) *Writing and Difference.* Chicago, The University of Chicago Press (translated from the French by Alan Bass).

Derrida, J. ([1972]/1993) *Dissemination.* London, The Athlone Press (translated from the French by Barbara Johnson).

Dessent, A. (1996) *Options for Partnership between Health, Education and Social Services.* Tamworth, National Association for Special Educational Needs.

DeVault, M. I., Harnischfeger, A. and Wiley, D. E. (1997) *Curricula, Personal Resources and Grouping Strategies.* St. Ann, MO, MI-GROUP for Policy Studies in Education, Central Midwestern Regional Lab.

Dewey, D. and Tupper, D. E. (eds) (2004) *Developmental Motor Disorders: A Neuropsychological Perspective.* New York, The Guilford Press.

Doll, R. C. (1996) (9th edition) *Curriculum Improvement: Decision Making and Process.* Needham Heights, MA, Allyn and Bacon.

Drake, R. F. (1996) 'A critique of the role of the traditional charities', in Barton, L. (ed.) *Disability and Society: Emerging Issues and Insights.* Harlow, Longman.

Drolet, M. (ed.) (2004) *The Postmodern Reader: Foundational Texts.* London and New York, Routledge.

Dyson, A. (2001) 'Special needs in the twenty-first century: where we've been and where we're going', *British Journal of Special Education,* **28**(1), 24–9.

Eagleton, T. (1996) (2nd edition) *Literary Theory: An Introduction.* Oxford, UK and Malden, MA, Blackwell.

Eayrs, C., Ellis, N. and Jones, R. (1993) 'Which label? An investigation into the effects of terminology on public perceptions of and attitudes towards people with learning difficulties', *Disability, Handicap and Society,* **8**(2), 111–28.

Editorial British Medical Journal (2004) 'Benefits and harms of drug treatments: observational studies and randomised trials should learn from each other', *British Medical Journal,* **329**, 2–3.

Editorial, Lancet (2004) 'Depressing research', *The Lancet*, **363**, 1335.

Esbensen, F. A. and Osgood, D. W. (1999) 'Gang resistance education and training (GREAT): Results from the national evaluation', *Journal of Research in Crime and Delinquency*, **36**, 194–225.

Farrell, M. (1990) 'The "new" criminology', *The Criminologist*, **4**(1), 46–7 (Spring).

Farrell, M. (1998) 'New terms for old', *The SLD Experience*, **21**, 16–17 (Summer).

Farrell, M. (1999) *Key Issues for Primary Schools*. London, Routledge.

Farrell, M. (2001a) *Key Issues for Secondary Schools*. London, Routledge.

Farrell, M. (2001b) *Standards and Special Educational Needs*. London, Continuum.

Farrell, M. (2003a) *Understanding Special Educational Needs: A Guide for Student Teachers*. New York and London, Routledge.

Farrell, M. (2003b) 'The role of the physiotherapist and occupational therapist', *Croner Special Educational Needs Briefing*, **22**, 1–4.

Farrell, M. (2004a) *Special Educational Needs: A Resource for Practitioners*. London, Sage.

Farrell, M. (2004b) *Inclusion at the Crossroads: Concepts and Values in Special Education*. London, David Fulton.

Farrell, M. (2005a) *The Effective Teacher's Guide to Dyslexia and Other Specific Learning Difficulties*. London, Routledge.

Farrell, M. (2005b) *The Effective Teacher's Guide to Moderate, Severe and Profound Learning Difficulties*. London, Routledge.

Farrell, M. (2005c) *The Effective Teacher's Guide to Autism and Communication Difficulties*. London, Routledge.

Farrell, M. (2005d) *The Effective Teacher's Guide to Sensory Impairment and Physical Disabilities*. London, Routledge.

Farrell, M. (2005e) *The Effective Teacher's Guide to Behavioural, Emotional and Social Difficulties*. London, Routledge.

Farrell, M. (2005f) *Key Issues in Special Education: Raising Pupils' Achievement and Attainment*. New York and London, Routledge.

Farrell, M. (2005g) 'Speech and language therapy', *Croner Special Educational Needs Briefing*, **37**, 2–4.

Farrell, M. (2006a) *Celebrating the Special School*. London, David Fulton.

Farrell, M. (2006b) 'Professionals working for pupils with SEN', *Croner Special Educational Needs Briefing*, **39**, 2–4.

Farrell, M. (2006c) 'A vision for inclusion', *Croner Special Educational Needs Briefing*, **45**, 2–4.

Farrell, M. (2008a) *Educating Special Children: An Introduction to Provision for Pupils with Disabilities and Disorders*. New York and London, Routledge.

Farrell, M. (2008b) *The Special School's Handbook: Key Issues for All*. London, Routledge/National Association for Special Education.

Farrell, M. (2009a) *Foundations of Special Education: An Introduction*. New York and London, Wiley.

Farrell, M. (2009b) (4th edition) *The Special Education Handbook*. London and New York, Routledge.

Farrell, M., Kerry, T. and Kerry, C. (1995) *The Blackwell Handbook of Education*. Oxford, Blackwell.

Fletcher, J. M., Shaywitz, S. E. and Shaywitz, B. A. (1999) 'Comorbidity of learning and attention disorders: separate but equal', *Paediatric Clinics of North America*, **46**, 885–897.

Fletcher, J. M., Morris, R. D. and Lyon, G. R. (2003) 'Classification and definition of learning disabilities: an integrative perspective', in Swanson, H. L., Harris, K. R. and Graham, S. (eds) (2003) *Handbook of Learning Disabilities*. New York, The Guilford Press.

Florian, L. and McLaughlin, M. J. (2008) *Disability Classification in Education: Issues and Perspectives*. Thousand Oaks, CA, Corwin Press.

Fonagy, P., Target, M., Cottrell, D., Phillips, J. and Kurtz, Z. (2005) *What Works for Whom? A Critical Review of Treatments for Children and Adolescents*. New York, The Guilford Press.

Forness, S. R., Kavale, K. A., Blum, I. M., and Lloyd, J. W. (1997). Mega-analysis of meta-analysis: what works in special education. *Teaching Exceptional Children*, 19(6), 4–9.

Foucault, M. ([1961]/2006) *The History of Madness*. London and New York, Routledge (translated from the French by Jonathan Murphy and Jean Khalfa).

Foucault, M. ([1963]/2003) *The Birth of the Clinic: An Archaeology of Medical Perception*. London and New York, Routledge Classics (translated from the French by A. M. Sheridan-Smith).

Foucault, M. ([1966]/2002) *The Order of Things: An Archaeology of the Human Sciences*. New York and London, Routledge Classics (translated from the French by an uncredited translator).

Foucault, M. ([1969]/2002) *The Archaeology of Knowledge*. London, Routledge Classics (translated from the French by A. M. Sheridan-Smith).

Foucault, M. ([1975]/1991) *Discipline and Punish: The Birth of the Prison*. New York and London, Penguin Books (translated from the French by Allan Sheridan).

Foucault, M. ([1976]/1998) *The History of Sexuality, Volume 1: The Will to Knowledge*. London and New York, Penguin Books (translated from the French by Robert Hurley).

Foucault, M. ([various dates]/1980) *Power/Knowledge: Selected Interviews and Other Writings 1972–1977* (ed. Gordon, C). New York, Pantheon.

Franklin, M. E., Kozak, M. J., Cashman, L. A., Coles, M. E., Rhiengold, A. A. and Foa, E. B. (1998) 'Cognitive-behavioural treatment of paediatric obsessive-compulsive disorder: an open clinic trial', *Journal of the American Academy of Child and Adolescent Psychiatry*, 37, 412–19.

Fulcher, G. (1989) *Disabling Policies? A Comparative Approach to Education Policy and Disability*. Lewes, UK, The Falmer Press.

Fulcher, G. (1995) 'Excommunicating the severely disabled: struggles, policy and researching', in Clough, P. and Barton, L (eds) *Making Difficulties: Research and the Construction on SEN*, London, Paul Chapman Publishing.

Gabbard, C. LeBlanc, B. and Lowry, S. (1994) (2nd edition) *Physical Education for Children: Building the Foundation*. Upper Saddle River NJ, Prentice-Hall.

Gallagher, D. J. (1998) 'The scientific knowledge base of special education: Do we know what we think we know?' *Exceptional Children*, 64, 493–502.

Gallagher, D. J. (2001) 'Neutrality as a moral standpoint, conceptual confusion and the full inclusion debate', *Disability and Society*, 16(5), 637–54.

Gardner, H. (1983) *Frames of Mind: The Theory of Multiple Intelligences*. New York, Basic Books.

Gardner, H. (1999) *Intelligence Reframed: Multiple Intelligences for the 21st Century*. New York, Basic Books.

Garland, E. J. (2004) 'Facing the evidence: anti-depressant treatment in children and adolescents', *Canadian Medical Journal*, 170, 489–91.

Gerber, M. M. (1994) 'Postmodernism in Special Education', *The Journal of Special Education*, 28(3), 368–78.

Ghia, A. (2002) 'Disability in the Indian context: post-colonial perspectives', in Corker, M. and Shakespeare, T. (eds) *Disability/Postmodernity: Embodying Disability Theory*. New York and London, Continuum.

Giedd, J. N., Blumenthal, J., Molloy, E. and Castellanos, F. X. (2001) 'Brain imaging of attention deficit/hyperactivity disorder', in Wassertein, J., Wolf, L. E. and Lefever, F. F. (eds) *Adult Attention Deficit Disorder: Brain Mechanisms and Life Outcomes*. New York, Annals of the New York Academy of Sciences, 931, 33-49

Gillberg, C. and Soderstrom, H. (2003) 'Learning disability', *The Lancet*, 362, 8711–821.

Gillman, M. Heyman, B. and Swain, J. (2000) 'What's in a name? The implications of diagnosis for people with learning difficulties and their family carers', *Disability and Society*, **15**(3), 389–409.

Glendon, M. (1991) *Rights Talk: The Impoverishment of Political Discourse*. New York, The Free Press.

Goodley, D. and Rapley, M. (2002) 'Changing the subject: post modernism and people with 'learning difficulties', in Corker, M. and Shakespeare, T. (eds) *Disability/Postmodernity: Embodying Disability Theory*. London, Continuum.

Gottlieb, J. (1986) 'Mainstreaming: fulfilling the promise?' *American Journal of Mental Deficiency*, **86**(2) 115–26.

Gould, S. J. (1987) *An Urchin in the Storm*. New York, W. W. Norton.

Gould, S. J. (1997) (2nd edition) *The Mismeasure of Man*. Harmondsworth, Penguin.

Greenhill, L. (1998) 'Childhood ADHD: pharmacological treatments', in Nathan, P. and Gorman, M. (eds) *A Guide to Treatments that Work*. Oxford, Oxford University Press.

Greenspan, S. (2006) 'Functional concepts in mental retardation: finding the natural essence of an artificial category', *Exceptionality*, **14**(4), 205–24.

Gross, P. R. (1998) 'The Icarian impulse', *The Wilson Quarterly*, **22**, 39–49.

Habermas, J. (1980) 'Modernity versus postmodernity', *New German Critique*, 22, Winter (translated from the German by Seyla Ben-Habi).

Habermas, J. (1985) *The Philosophical Discourse of Modernity: Twelve Lectures*. Cambridge, Polity Press (translated from the German by Frederick G. Lawrence).

Hale, J. B. and Fiorello, C. A. (2004) *School Neuropsychology: A Practitioner's Handbook*. New York, The Guilford Press.

Hargreaves, D. H. (1978) 'The proper study of educational psychology', *Association of Educational Psychologists Journal*, **4**(9), 3–8.

Hearnshaw, L. S. (1979) *Cyril Burt: Psychologis*. London, Hodder and Stoughton.

Herrnstein, R. J. and Murray, C. (1994) *The Bell Curve: Intelligence and Class Structure in American Life*. New York, The Free Press.

Heshusius, L. (1991) 'Curriculum-based assessment and direct instruction: critical reflections on fundamental assumptions', *Exceptional Children*, **57**, 315–29.

Heshusius, L. (2004) 'From creative discontent toward epistemological freedom in special education: reflections on a 25 year journey', in Gallagher, D. J., Heshusius, L., Iano, R. P. and Skrtic, T. M. (eds) (2004) *Challenging Orthodoxy in Special Education: Disseminating Voices*. Denver, CO, Love Publishing, pp. 169–230.

Hornby, G., Atkinson, M. and Howard, J. (1997) *Controversial Issues in Special Education*. London, David Fulton.

House of Commons Education and Skills Committee (2006) *Special Educational Needs: Third Report of Session 2005–6 Volume 1*. London, The Stationery Office.

Howe, M. (1997) *IQ in Question*. London, Sage Publications

Hughes, B., Russell, R. and Paterson, K. (2005) 'Nothing to be had 'off the peg': consumption, identity and mobilization of young disabled people', *Disability and Society*, **20** (1), 3–18.

Humphries, T. L. (2003) 'Effectiveness of pivotal response training as a behavioural intervention for young children with autism spectrum disorders', *Bridges Practice Based Research Synthesis*, **2**(4), 1–10.

Hurst, R. (2003) 'To revise or not to revise?' *Disability and Society*, **15**(7), 1083–7.

Hurt, J. (1988) *Outside the Mainstream: A History of Special Education*. London, Batsford.

Johnson, B. (1997) 'Translator's Introduction' to Jacques Derrida's *Dissemination*. London, The Athlone Press.

Johnson, M. and Parkinson, G. (2002) *Epilepsy: A Practical Guide*. London, David Fulton Publishers.

Jupp, K. (1992) *Everyone Belongs: Mainstream Education for Children with Severe Learning Difficulties*. Human Horizon Series, London, Souvenir Press.

Jureidini, J and Mansfield, P. (2006) 'The scope of the problem of the relationship between drug companies and doctors', in Timimi, S. and Maitra, B. (eds) *Critical Voices in Child and Adolescent Mental Health*. London, Free Association Books.

Kaplan, E., Fein, D., Kramer, J., Delis, D. and Morris, R. Wechsler, D. (2004) (4th edition) *Wechsler Intelligence Scale for Children ® (WISCIV) Integrated*. London, Pearson Assessment.

Kauffman, J. M. (1999) 'Commentary: today's special education and its messages for tomorrow', *The Journal of Special Education*, **32**(4), 244–54.

Kauffman, J. M. and Hallahan, D. P. (1995) *The Illusion of Full Inclusion: A Comprehensive Critique of a Current Special Education Bandwagon*. Austin, TX, PRO-ED.

Kavale, K. A. and Mostert, M. P. (2003) 'River of ideology, islands of evidence', *Exceptionality*, **11**(4), 191–208.

Kazdin, A.E. (2001) (5th edition) *Behavior Modification in Applied Settings*. Pacific Grove, CA, Brooks/Cole.

Kendall, P. C., Aschenbrand, S. G. and Hudson, J. L. (2003) 'Child focused treatment of anxiety', in Kazdin, A. E. and Weisz, T. R. (eds) (2003) *Evidence Based Psychotherapies for Children and Adolescents*. New York, The Guilford Press, pp. 81–100.

Kiel, D. C. (1995) 'The radical humanist view of special education and disability: consciousness, freedom and ideology', in Skrtic, T. M. (ed.) (1995) *Disability and Democracy: Reconstructing (Special) Education for Postmodernity*, New York, Teachers College Press, Colombia University.

King, N. J., Tonge, B. J., Heyne, D., Turner, S. M., Pritchard, M., Young, D. *et al.* (2001) 'Cognitive-behavioural treatment of school refusing children: maintenance of improvement at 3 to 5 year follow up', *Scandinavian Journal of Behaviour Therapy*, **30**, 85–9.

Kirigin, K. A. (1996) Teaching-Family model of group home treatment of children with severe behaviour problems' in Roberts, M. C. (ed.) *Model Programs in Child and Family Mental Health*. Mahwah, NJ, Erlbaum, pp. 231–47.

Knox J. E. and Stevens C. B. (1993) 'Translators' Introduction', in Rieber, R. W. and Carton, A. S. (eds) *The Collected Works of L. S. Vygotsky Volume 2: The Fundamentals of Defectology (Abnormal Psychology and Learning Disabilities)*. New York, Plenum Press.

Koegel, L. K. and Koegel, R. L. (1995) 'Motivating communication in children with autism', in Schopler, E. and Mezibov, G. (eds) *Learning and Cognition in Autism: Current Issues in Autism*. New York, Plenum Press, pp. 73–87.

Kundera, M. (1991) *Immortality*. London, Faber and Faber.

Kurtz, P. D., Harrison, M. Neisworth, J. T. and Jones, R. T. (1977) 'Influence of "mentally retarded" label on teachers' non-verbal behaviour towards pre-school children', *American Journal of Mental Deficiency*, **82**, 204–6.

Kushlick, A. and Blunden, R. (1974) 'The epidemiology of mental subnormality', in Clarke, A. M. and Clarke, A. D. B. (eds) *Mental Deficiency* (3rd edition). London, Methuen.

Lacey, P. (2000) 'Multidisciplinary work: challenges and possibilities', in Daniels, H. (ed.) *Special Education Re-formed: Beyond Rhetoric New Millennium Series*. London, Falmer Press.

Lane, H. (1984) *When the Mind Hears: A History of the Deaf*. New York, Random House.

Lewis, A. and Norwich, B. (eds) (2005) *Special Teaching for Special Children? Pedagogies for Inclusion*. Maidenhead, UK, Open University Press.

Lezak, M. D., Howieson, D. B. and Loring, D. W. (2004) (2nd edition) *Neuropsychological Assessment*. New York, Oxford University Press.

Lindsay, G. (2003) Inclusive education: a critical perspective', *British Journal of Special Education*, **3**(1), 3–12.

Litow, L. and Pumroy, D. K. (1975) 'A brief review of classroom group-orientated contingencies', *Journal of Applied Behavioural Analysis*, **3**, 341–7.

Lloyd, G., Stead, J. and Cohen, D. (eds) (2006) *Critical New Perspectives on ADHD*. New York, Routledge.

Lyotard, F. ([1979]/1984) *The Postmodern Condition: A Report on Knowledge*. Manchester, Manchester University Press (translated from the French by G. Bennington and B. Massumi).

Macey, D. (2000) *The Penguin Dictionary of Critical Theory*. London and New York, Penguin Books.

MacMillan, D. L., Jones, R. L. and Aloia, G. F. (1974) 'The mentally retarded label: a theoretical analysis and review of research', *American Journal of Mental Deficiency*, **79**, 241–61.

Manset, G. and Semmel, M. I. (1997) 'Are inclusive programmes for students with mild disabilities effective? A comparative review of model programmes', *Journal of Special Education*, **31**(2), 155–80.

Marston, D. (1996) 'A comparison of inclusion only, pull-out only, and combined service models for students with mild disabilities', *Journal of Special Education*, **30**(2), 121–32.

Mautner, T. (ed.) (2000) *The Penguin Dictionary of Philosophy*. London, Penguin Books.

Meighan, R. and Harber, C. (2007) *A Sociology of Educating*. London, Continuum.

Menzies, R. G. and Clarke, J. C. (1993) 'A comparison of in vivo and vicarious exposure in the treatment of childhood water phobia', *Behaviour Research and Therapy*, **31**, 9–15.

Mills, P. E., Cole, K. N., Jenkins, J. R. and Dale, P. S. (1998) 'Effects of differing levels of inclusion on pre-schoolers with disabilities', *Exceptional Children*, **65**, 79–90.

Minogue, K. (1995) *Politics: A Very Short Introduction*. Oxford, Oxford University Press.

Mitchell, D. (ed.) (2004a) *Special Educational Needs and Inclusive Education: Major Themes in Education, Volume 1: Systems and Contexts*. London and New York, Routledge Falmer.

Mitchell, D. (ed.) (2004b) *Special Educational Needs and Inclusive Education: Major Themes in Education, Volume 2: Inclusive Education*. London and New York, Routledge Falmer.

Mitchell, D. (ed.) (2004c) *Special Educational Needs and Inclusive Education: Major Themes in Education, Volume 3: Assessment and Teaching Strategies*. London and New York, Routledge Falmer.

Mitchell, D. (ed.) (2004d) *Special Educational Needs and Inclusive Education: Major Themes in Education, Volume 4: Effective Practices*. London and New York, Routledge Falmer.

Moffitt, T.E., Caspi, A, Harkness, R, and Silva, P. A. (1993) 'The natural history of change in intellectual performance: who changes? How much? Is it meaningful?', *Journal of Child Psychology and Psychiatry*, **34**, 455–506.

Morton, J. (2004) *Understanding Developmental Disorders: A Causal Modelling Approach*. Oxford, Blackwell Publishing.

Munden, A. and Arcelus, J. (1999) *The AD/HD Handbook*. London, Jessica Kingsley.

Muratori, F., Picchi, L., Casella, C., Tancredi, R., Milone, A. and Patarnello, M. G. (2002) 'Efficacy of brief dynamic psychotherapy for children with emotional disorders', *Psychotherapy and Psychosomatics*, **71**, 2838.

National Center on Inclusive Education and Restructuring (1995) *National Study of Inclusive Education*. New York, The City University of New York, NCIER.

National Institute of Clinical Excellence (2000) *Guidance on the Use of Methylphenidate for ADHD*. London, NICE.

Newcomer, P. I. and Hammill, D. D. (1975) 'ITPA and academic achievement', *Reading Teacher*, **28**, 731–42.

Norwich, B. (2008) 'Perspectives and purposes of disability classification systems: implications for teachers and curriculum pedagogy', in Florian, L. and McLaughlin, M. J. (2008) *Disability Classification in Education: Issues and Perspectives*. Thousand Oaks, CA, Corwin Press.

Norwich, B. and Kelly, N. (2004) *Moderate Learning Difficulties and the Future of Inclusion*. London, Routledge Falmer.

Nozick, R. (1974) *Anarchy, State and Utopia*. Oxford, Blackwell.

O'Leary, K. D. and Drabman, R. (1971) 'Token reinforcement programs in the classroom: a review', *Psychological Bulletin*, **75**, 379–98.

Oliver, M. (1992) 'Intellectual masturbation: a rejoinder to Soder and Booth', *European Journal of Special Needs Education*, **7**(1), 20–8.

Oliver, M. (1995) 'Does special education have a role to play in the 21st century?' *REACH, Journal of Special Needs Education in Ireland*, **8**(2), 67–76.

Ollendick, T. H. and King, N. J. (1998) 'Empirically supported treatments for children with phobic and anxiety disorders', *Journal of Clinical Child Psychology*, **27**, 156–67.

Orlowski, J. P. and Wateska, L. (1992) 'The effects of pharmaceutical firm enticements on physician prescribing patterns: there's no such thing as a free lunch', *Chest* (Journal of American College of Chest Physicians), **102**, 270–3.

Peetsma, T., Verger, M., Roeleveld, J. and Karsten, S. (2001) 'Inclusion in education: comparing pupil's development in special education and regular education', *Education Review*, **53**(2), 125–35.

Peterkin T. (2004) 'Feudal laird prepares for battle with islanders who want to buy him out', *The Daily Telegraph*, Tuesday 1 June 2004.

Peters, R. S. (1966) *Ethics and Education*. London, Allen and Unwin.

Pierce, W. D. and Cheney, C. D. (2008) (4th edition) *Behaviour Analysis and Learning*. New York, Psychology Press.

Powers, S., Gregory, S. and Thoutonhoofd, D. (1999) 'The educational achievement of deaf children', *Deafness and Education International*, **1**(1), 1–9.

Pritchard, D. G. (1963) *Education of the Handicapped 1760–1960*. London, Routledge and Kegan Paul.

Rajchman, J. (1991) *Truth and Eros: Foucault, Lacan, and the Question of Ethics*. New York, Routledge.

Raven, J. C. *et al.* (1998) *Raven's Progressive Matrices and Vocablary Scales*. London, San Antonio, TX, Pearson.

Rawls, J. (1971) *A Theory of Justice*. Cambridge, MA, Harvard University Press.

Rebar, M. (2007) 'Academic acceleration in first grade using the direct instruction model (Report No. 2007–1)'. Cheney, WA: Eastern Washington University.

Reiser, R. and Mason, M. (1992) *Disability Equality in the Classroom: A Human Rights Issue*. London, Disability Equality in Education.

Richardson, K. (1999) *The Making of Intelligence*. London, Weidenfeld and Nicolson.

Riddle, M. A., Reeve, A. E., Yaryura-Tobias, J. A. *et al.* (2001) 'Fluvoxamine for children and adolescents with obsessive-compulsive disorder: a randomised, controlled, multicenter trail', *Journal of the American Academy of Child and Adolescent Psychiatry*, **40**, 222–9.

Roaf, C. and Bines, H. (1989) 'Needs, rights and opportunities in special education', in Chitty, C. (ed.) *Redefining the Comprehensive Experience (Bedford Way Papers 32)*. London, University Institute of Education.

Rose, S., Lewontin, R. C. and Kamin, L. J. (1984) *Not in Our Genes*. London, Penguin.

Rutherford, R. B. Jr and Nelson, C. M. (1982) 'Analysis of response contingent time-out literature with behaviourally disordered students in classroom settings', in Rutherford, R. B. Jr (ed.) *Severe Behaviour Disorders of Children and Youth*, Volume 5 (pp. 79–105). Reston, VA, Council for Children with Behavioural Disorders.

Rutherford, R. B. Jr and Polsgrove, L. J. (1981) 'Behavioural contracting with behaviourally disordered and delinquent children and youth: An analysis of the clinical and experimental literature', in Rutherford, R. B. Jr, Prieto, A. G. and McGlothlin, J. E. (eds) *Severe Behaviour Disorders of Children and Youth*, Volume 4 (pp. 49–69). Reston, VA, Council for Children with Behavioural Disorders.

Ryder, R. J., Burton, J. L., and Silberg, A. (2006) 'Longitudinal study of direct instruction effects from first through third grade', *Journal of Educational Research*, **99**(3), 179–91.

Safford, P. L. and Safford, E. J. (1996) *A History of Childhood and Disability*. New York, Teachers College Press.

Salend, S. J. and Duhany, L. M. G. (1999) 'The impact of inclusion on students with and without disabilities and their educators', *Remedial and Special Education*, **20**(2), 114–26.

Sapsted, D. (2004) 'TV is human right says tree row man', *The Daily Telegraph*, 31 May 2004, News page 6 columns 6–7.

Sasso, G. M. (2001) 'The retreat from inquiry and knowledge in special education', *The Journal of Special Education*, **34**(4), 178–93.

Schoenbrodt, L. (ed.) (2001) *Children with Traumatic Brain Injury: A Parent's Guide*. Bethesda, MD, Woodbine House.

Schweinhart, L. J. and Welkhart, D. P. (1997) 'Lasting difference: the high/scope preschool curriculum comparison through age 23', *Early Childhood Research Quarterly*, **12**, 117–43.

Shakespeare, T. (2006) *Disability Rights and Wrongs*. London and New York, Routledge.

Shakespeare, T. and Erickson, M. (2000) 'Different strokes: beyond biological essentialism and social constructionism', in Rose, S. and Rose, H. (eds) *Coming to Life*. New York, Little Brown.

Simeonson, R. J., Simeonson, N. E. and Hollenweger, J. (2008) 'International classification of functioning, disability and health for children and youth', in Florian, L. and McLaughlin, M. J. (2008) *Disability Classification in Education: Issues and Perspectives*. Thousand Oaks, CA, Corwin Press.

Simpson, R. L. (2005) 'Evidence based practices and students with ASD', *Focus on Autism and Other Developmental Disabilities*, **20**(3), 140–49.

Skidmore, D. (2004) *Inclusion: The Dynamic of School Development*. Buckingham, UK, Open University Press/McGraw-Hill Education.

Skrtic, T. (1991) *Behind Special Education: A Critical Analysis of Professional Culture and School Organization*. Denver, CO, Love Publishing Company.

Skrtic, T. M. (1995a) 'The functionalist view of special education and disability: deconstructing the conventional knowledge tradition', in Skrtic, T. M. (ed.) *Disability and Democracy: Reconstructing (Special) Education for Post-modernity*. New York, Teachers College Press.

Skrtic, T. M. (1995b) (ed.) *Disability and Democracy: Reconstructing (Special) Education for Post-modernity*. New York, Teachers College Press.

Soanes, C. and Stevenson, A. (eds) (2003) (2nd edition) *Oxford Dictionary of English*. Oxford, Oxford University Press.

Sokal, A. and Bricmont, J. ([1997]/1999). *Intellectual Impostures: Postmodern Philosophers' Abuse of Science*. London, Profile Books (translated from the original French by the authors).

Sokal, A. and Bricmont, J. (1998) *Fashionable Nonsense: Postmodern Intellectuals' Abuse of Science*. New York, Picador.

Sparrow, S. S., Chicchetti, D. V. and Balla, D. A. (2006) (2nd edition) *Vineland Adaptive Behaviour Scales* (Vineland II). London, Pearson Assessments.

Stanovich, P. J., Jordan, A., Perot, J. (1998) 'Relative differences in academic self concept and peer acceptance among students in inclusive classrooms', *Remedial and Special Education*, **19**(2), 120–6.

Steiner, G. (1971) 'The mandarin of the hour – Michel Foucault', *The New York Times*, 28 February.

Swain, J. and French, S. (2000) 'Towards and affirmation model of disability', *Disability and Society*, **15**(4), 569–82.

Swanson, J. M., Lerner, M. and Williams, L. (1995) 'More frequent diagnosis of ADHD', *New England Journal of Medicine*, **333**, 944.

Thomas, G. and Loxley, A. (2007) (2nd edition) *Deconstructing Special Education and Constructing Inclusion*. Maidenhead, UK, Open University Press/McGraw-Hill.

Thomas, G. and Vaughan, M. (2004) *Inclusive Education: Readings and Reflections*. Buckingham, UK, Open University Press/McGraw-Hill Education.

Timimi, S. (2006) 'Childhood depression?' in Timimi, S. and Maitra, B. (eds) (2006) *Critical Voices in Child and Adolescent Mental Health*. London, Free Association Books.

Timimi, S. and Maitra, B. (eds) (2006) *Critical Voices in Child and Adolescent Mental Health*. London, Free Association Books.

Tomlinson, S. (1982) *A Sociology of Special Education*. London, Routledge and Kegan Paul.

Thompson, N. (2001) (3rd edition) *Anti-Discriminatory Practice*. Basingstoke, UK, Palgrave.

Tolson, J. (1998) At issue: the many and the one', *The Wilson Quarterly*, **22**, 12.

Toren, P., Wolmer, L., Rosental, B. *et al.* (2000) 'Case series: brief parent–child group therapy for childhood anxiety disorders using a manual based cognitive-behavioural technique', *Journal of the American Academy for Child and Adolescent Psychiatry*, **39**(10), 1309–12.

Tremain, S. (2002) 'On the subject of impairment', in Corker, M. and Shakespeare, T. (eds) *Disability/Postmodernity: Embodying Disability Theory*. London, Continuum.

United Nations, *Convention on the Rights of the Child* (adopted by General Assembly resolution 44/25 on 20 November 1989).

United Nations Educational, Scientific and Cultural Organization, *The Salamanca Statement and Framework for Action on Special Needs Education* (adopted by the World Conference on Special Needs Education: Access and Quality in Salamanca, Spain, 10 June, 1994).

Vaughan, S. and Klinger, J. K. (1998) 'Students' perceptions of inclusion and resource room settings', *Journal of Special Education*, **32**(2), 79–88.

Vlachou, A. D. (1997) *Struggles for Inclusive Education: An Ethnographic Study*. Buckingham, UK, Open University Press/McGraw-Hill Education.

Vygotsky, L. S. ([1924]/1993) 'The psychology and pedagogy of children's handicaps' (originally published in *Questions of Education of the Blind, the Deaf–Mute and Mentally Retarded Children* edited by Vygotsky, 1929), in Rieber, R. W. and Carton, A. S. (eds) (1993) *The Collected Works of L. S. Vygotsky Volume 2: The Fundamentals of Defectology (Abnormal Psychology and Learning Disabilities)* (translation by Knox, J. E. and Stevens, C. B.). New York, Plenum Press.

Vygotsky, L. S. ([1925–6]/1993) 'Principles of education for physically handicapped children' (based on a report of the same title prepared for the Second Congress on the Social and Legal Protection of Minors, 1924), in Rieber, R. W. and Carton, A. S. (eds) (1993) *The Collected Works of L. S. Vygotsky Volume 2: The Fundamentals of Defectology (Abnormal Psychology and Learning Disabilities)* (translation by Knox, J. E. and Stevens, C. B.). New York, Plenum Press.

Vygotsky, L. S. ([1927]/1993) 'Defect and compensation' (a version was published as 'Defect and Overcompensation' in *Retardation, Blindness and Deafness*, 1927), in Rieber, R. W. and Carton, A. S. (eds) (1993) *The Collected Works of L. S. Vygotsky Volume 2: The Fundamentals of Defectology (Abnormal Psychology and Learning Disabilities)* (translation by Knox, J. E. and Stevens, C. B.). New York, Plenum Press.

Vygotsky, L. S. ([various dates]/1978) *Mind in Society: The Development of Higher Psychological Processes*, Cole, M., John-Steiner, V., Scribner, S. and Souberman, E. (eds). Cambridge, MA, Harvard University Press.

Walker, H. M. (1983) 'Application of response cost in school settings: outcomes, issues and recommendations', *Exceptional Children Quarterly*, 3(4), 46–55.

Walker, S. (2007) 'Labelling theory and life chances', in Meighan, R. and Harber, C. (eds) *A Sociology of Educating*. London, Continuum.

Ware, J. (2003) *Creating a Responsive Environment for People with Profound and Multiple Learning Difficulties*. London, David Fulton Publishers.

Warnock, M. (2006) 'Foreword', in Farrell, M. (2006) *Celebrating the Special School*. London, David Fulton.

Wertheimer, A. (1997) *Inclusive Education: A Framework for Change. National and International Perspectives*. Bristol, Centre for Studies in Inclusive Education.

Wertsch, J. V. (1985) *Vygotsky and the Social Formation of Mind*. Cambridge, MA, Harvard University Press.

Whitaker, S. (1996) 'A review of DRO: The influence of the degree of intellectual disability and the frequency of the target behaviour', *Journal of Applied Research in Intellectual Disabilities*, 9, 61–79.

White, W. A. T. (1988). 'Meta-analysis of the effects of direct instruction in special education', *Education and Treatment of Children*, 11, 364–74.

Wilmot, G. (2006) 'Educational inclusion and special schooling within a local education authority,' thesis for the degree of Doctor of Education, University of Birmingham.

Wittgenstein, L. ([1945]/2001) *Philosophical Investigations* (the German text with English translation by G. E. M. Anscombe).Oxford, Blackwell.

World Health Organization (2002) *International Classification of Functioning, Disability and Health: Towards a Common Language for Functioning, Disability and Health*. Geneva, WHO.

World Health Organization (2007) *International Classification of Functioning, Disability and Health: Children and Youth Version*. Geneva, WHO.

Index